The Course
of
Human History

Sources
and
Studies
in World
History

Kevin Reilly, Series Editor

THE ALCHEMY OF HAPPINESS
Abu Hamid Muhammad al-Ghazzali
translated by Claud Field, revised and annotated by Elton L. Daniel

LIFELINES FROM OUR PAST
A New World History
L. S. Stavrianos

NATIVE AMERICANS BEFORE 1492
The Moundbuilding Centers of the Eastern Woodlands
Lynda Norene Shaffer

GERMS, SEEDS, AND ANIMALS
Studies in Ecological History
Alfred W. Crosby

BALKAN WORLDS
The First and Last Europe
Traian Stoianovich

AN ATLAS AND SURVEY OF
SOUTH ASIAN HISTORY
Karl J. Schmidt

THE GOGO: HISTORY, CUSTOMS, AND TRADITIONS
Mathias E. Mnyampala
Translated, introduced, and edited by Gregory H. Maddox

WOMEN IN WORLD HISTORY:
Volume 1—Readings from Prehistory to 1500
Volume 2—Readings from 1500 to the Present
Sarah Shaver Hughes and Brady Hughes

MARITIME SOUTHEAST ASIA TO 1500
Lynda Norene Shaffer

THE COURSE OF HUMAN HISTORY
Economic Growth, Social Process, and Civilization
Johan Goudsblom, Eric Jones, and Stephen Mennell

The Course of Human History

Economic Growth, Social Process, and Civilization

Johan Goudsblom, Eric Jones,
and Stephen Mennell

M.E. Sharpe

Armonk, New York
London, England

Library of Congress Cataloging-in-Publication Data

The course of human history : economic growth, social process, and civilization /
Johan Goudsblom, Eric Jones, and Stephen Mennell.
p.   cm. —
(Sources and studies in world history)
Includes bibliographical references and index.
ISBN 1-56324-793-3 (hardcover : alk. paper). —
ISBN 1-56324-794-1 (paperback : alk. paper)
1. Culture.
2. Civilization.
3. Progress.
4. Social evolution.
5. Social change.
6. Economic development.
I. Jones, E. L. (Eric Lionel)
II. Mennell, Stephen.
III. Title.
IV. Series.
HM101.G675   1996
306—dc20 96-4547
CIP

Printed in the United States of America

The paper used in this publication meets the minimum requirements of the
American National Standard for Information Sciences—
Permanence of Paper for Printed Library Materials,
ANSI Z 39.48-1984.

BM (c)   10   9   8   7   6   5   4   3   2   1
BM (p)   10   9   8   7   6   5   4   3   2   1

On the Cover: Ancient Gerasa with modern Jerash (N. Jordan) in the background.
Courtesy of Kevin Reilly, Series Editor.

Contents

Foreword

These essays offer routes to world history that are rarely traveled by historians. They are high mountain roads, from which one can see great distances. The authors call these broad vistas "long-term historical processes." The essays are the product of an unusual collaboration—a seminar on "Very Long-Term Economic and Social Processes," taught jointly at the University of Exeter by Stephen Mennell (now of University College Dublin), Johan Goudsblom (University of Amsterdam), and Eric Jones (University of Melbourne). Johan Goudsblom and Stephen Mennell are sociologists, influenced by the historical sociology of Norbert Elias. With Elias they revisit and revive the great traditions of Victorian social evolutionists Herbert Spencer, Edward B. Tylor, and Sir Henry Sumner Maine, and the historical sociology of Max Weber, all of whom pointed a way to world history a century ago.

Johan Goudsblom, who has previously written in *Fire and Civilization* about one of the most formative developments in human history, here discusses agrarian regimes from the neolithic revolution to the modern era. The dominant social process of these regimes, Goudsblom argues, is to create first priests and organized religion and then soldiers and military regimes. Skipping across millennia, he urges us to be guided by "phaseology" as well as chronology but to be warned that dominant trends often produce countertrends.

Stephen Mennell deals directly with the work of Norbert Elias. He explores the utility of Elias's notions of "civilizing" and "decivilizing" processes for an understanding of world history. While Elias concentrates on European, especially French, history, Mennell offers a framework for comparing these long-term social processes in European and Asian history.

The third author, Eric Jones, is an economist and economic historian, already familiar to world historians for such works as *The European Miracle* and *Growth Recurring*. In the latter work and the essays here, Jones suggests a new paradigm of economic history. Instead of marking all history from the vantage point of the Western Industrial

Revolution, Jones suggests a focus on the ways in which "extensive growth" has become "intensive growth" in a number of different historical societies, including Song China and Tokugawa Japan as well as early modern Europe.

Essays like these argue (to use Goudsblom's formulation) the value of "conceiving of the human past not in terms of the names and dates of individuals but in terms of impersonal stages or phases." These essays remind us that greater detail does not always produce greater knowledge. Jones, for instance, points out that the array of historical research on British industrialization has informed us only of "fellow passengers, correlates, not causes" of economic growth. Further, an exclusive study of Britain has distracted our attention from the larger issues of economic growth that only a comparative approach can grasp.

Not all issues are resolved here (nor could they be). To conceive of the past as stages or phases is not entirely consistent with the emphasis on process. The most venerable stage theory of world history—hunting/gathering, followed by agricultural, followed by industrial society—is crucial to Goudsblom but challenged by Jones. All authors agree, however, that historians need phases that are not fixed and processes that are not constant. Similarly, while Mennell looks to Asia for civilizing processes on the European model and Jones explicitly rejects the European model of industrialization, both authors recognize the need to avoid the Eurocentrism of the founders of historical sociology. Together these essays stimulate us to look at the entire course of human history, sometimes in a fresh new light.

Kevin Reilly

The Course
of
Human History

Introduction

Bringing the Very Long Term Back In

Stephen Mennell

For many years, an interest in the long-term development of human society was faintly disreputable among both historians and sociologists. The very long term, however, has lately received distinctly new attention. This book is the outcome of collaboration between three authors—one economic historian and two sociologists—whose concern with long-term processes is of long standing.

Our common purpose is to explain the origins and development of major features of human society: priests and organized religion, military men, economic expansion and economic growth, civilizing and decivilizing processes. These deep processes are each set in ecological and historical context. Together they contribute to an account of human history as an overlapping series of rationally explicable but unintended processes fundamental to the formation of modern society.

The book opens with Johan Goudsblom's restatement of the case for the study of long-term social processes in human history. Sociologists and historians have long been haunted by the ghosts of Herbert Spencer and other Victorian social evolutionists who, in attempting to put their own society and its recent transformation in the perspective of the history of humanity as a whole, actually succeeded only in putting the whole history of humanity in the perspective of their own society. Goudsblom advocates a synthesis of chronology and "phaseology" in a way which retains all the important questions posed by the old social evolutionists while avoiding the pitfalls into which their answers stumbled. Underlying the argument is a distinctive conception of the type of theory which sociologists and historians ought to be striving to construct: "process theories."[1] As Goudsblom writes, "The processes come into the foreground, with 'phases' or 'stages' no longer defined as stationary states but in terms of the very processes of which they are a part and through which they are generated" (pages 21–22 below). Traditional thinking in terms of a few causal "variables" or "factors" also rests on a reduction of processes to a sequence of static phases. That a similar quest for process theories underlies Eric Jones's thinking is evident when he writes of the search for prime movers in industrialization:

> Models of growth usually assume the success of one or another novel force. The postwar experience of the Third World is, however, a graveyard of hopes that some particular propellant might be effective. Earlier British economic historiography is similarly a cemetery for an array of suggested push forces or positive shocks, none of them fully capable of accounting for growth in its industrial guise, let alone as a general process. (Page 89 below.)

The meat in the sandwich of this book consists of two chapters by Goudsblom and two by Jones, having in common a principal focus on agrarian societies. That is to say, they are concerned with human society in the course of, and following, its second great ecological transformation—"second" because, as Goudsblom has shown in his book *Fire and Civilization* (1992b), the first and neglected great transformation was the domestication of fire. In chapters 2 and 3, he deals with the sociogenesis in agrarian societies of priests and warriors respectively. In an argument which avoids teleology, he shows how both of these great historic roles originated out of a compelling necessity for coordinated effort, which itself is a necessity in the achievement of both extensive and intensive growth.

After Goudsblom's studies of priests and warriors comes Eric Jones's case for a very long-term and global economic history; long-term economic growth provides the context for so many other long-term social processes.[2] Jones's argument is in two sections. First, in chapter 4, he urges that the *very* long-term historical record is of economic expansion, called *extensive* growth. In other words, economic output and total income were rising in pace with population growth. One implication is that there were continual investment decisions and continual positive economic activity. Although, over thousands of years before the present, this aggregate growth was seldom strong enough to overtake the rise in population so as to produce rising average (as opposed to total) income, it had important consequences. Most significant is its role in the historical transitions (note the plural) to economic growth as it is normally understood: *intensive* growth, the rise of real income per head. Jones deals with these transitions in chapter 5. *Intensive* growth did not burst suddenly and only once on a uniformly dreary world of stagnation, but emerged within the context of existing economic expansion. As Jones has argued in his earlier works, so-called "modern" economic growth was not inherently as improbable as it is usually regarded to be. The technical and cultural barriers, though steep, were simply not as intractable as writings on economic development and much of the literature on economic history assumes. Once the process of *intensive* growth starts, it can overcome the worst of these difficulties relatively smoothly. The central diffi-, culty lies elsewhere—Jones thinks in the realm of politics. RENT-SEEKING

Essentially, Jones is starting with the simple, rather stark, behavioral assumption that—other things being equal—enough individuals in any large society will try to reduce their own material poverty. A largely unintended consequence of this impulse, as it is aggregated, is the expansion of the economy. Left to accumulate, there is no reason intrinsic to economic motivations why this expansion should not be sufficiently rapid to overtake the growth of population, thus producing *intensive* growth, rising incomes per head.

Why, then, does such a smooth transition often not work? The social process for our species may after all have been one of *extensive* growth rather than stagnation, but it has patently not been one of *intensive* growth since the beginning of human history. Yet one of Eric Jones's key observations is that there has been more than one transition from expansion to income growth. The trick is to explain the transitions. Here the argument is not that growth was positively caused, but that circumstances removed obstacles to it and permitted it to unfold. This thesis is methodologically convergent with Goudsblom's approach to the sociogenesis of priests and warriors. The forces which have operated throughout most of history to select *against* the common impulse to growth do, from time to time, weaken and move into reverse. If this reversal lasts long enough, the "technical" or purely economic barriers will be overcome and a prolonged process of growth will set in. Usually this does not happen because a competing impulse is present: a compulsive tendency of elites toward rent-seeking, which amounts to using political means to capture the surplus produced by others, rather than using directly "economic" activities in the pursuit of wealth.

In Jones's view, the significant "windows" through which a handful of societies have passed have themselves been the unintended results of fortunate stalemates when political elites have canceled out each other's capacity fully to acquire the surplus, and may indeed have begun to compete with one another in offering services with which to retain relatively wide political support (Jones, 1990a). This probably characterizes the European and Japanese cases.

A second route—"emergency marketization"—is suggested by interesting work by S.R.H. Jones (1988) on the regime of Alfred the Great. An occasional government, instead of pursuing the customary route of squeezing wealth out of its subjects, frees factor markets and encourages commerce in the hope of providing revenues to meet a common foe. History, after all, offers multiple experiments, and every so often there appears a ruler such as Alfred. In Eric Jones's outline, the case of intensive growth which may turn out to fall into this second category of "emergency marketization" is that of Song China, beset by the Tartar hordes.

In sum, the sequence as Jones envisages it involves the removal, by one of two mechanisms, of the forces commonly selecting against growth and certainly capable of restraining transitions to growth of the *intensive* variety.

One of Jones's major objectives is to provide a model which will at one and the same time encompass the earlier history of both the Western and Eastern growth poles so evident in the modern world. The history of *intensive* growth is not the same as the history of industrialization, or of capitalism, or of democracy, or of the rise of the West. In the West, all these *were* interwoven in a spiral process. But once one has conceptually fused all these together, it becomes difficult to extricate them. East Asia challenges this melding: the spiral there is not necessarily at all the same spiral as in the West.

Despite our different disciplinary affiliations, the three authors share a good deal of common ground. We share a skepticism about the traditional economic history, heavily Eurocentric with its strong emphasis on an apparently unique sequence of events starting in Lancashire on 1 January 1760.

We also share a common attitude toward evidence and explanation. In particular we share a suspicion of all forms of mentalistic explanation, where culture, religion, or ideology is seen as the main engine of history. This may come across in what we have written as a hostility toward explanations derived from the work of Max Weber. Whether Weber himself can be blamed for the way his work has been used since his death is questionable. In his defense, it can be said that he was himself reacting against idealistic explanations in the German tradition, as well as against the vulgar "Second International" Marxism of his time. As he remarked in the last paragraph of *The Protestant Ethic and the Spirit of Capitalism,* "it is not my aim to substitute for a one-sided materialistic an equally one-sided spiritualistic causal interpretation of culture and of history" (1930 [1904-5], 183). Too often, the legacy of his work, especially in the anglophone academic world, has been to cause sociologists great excitement whenever they spy anything remotely resembling a Protestant ethic, to be too willing—in our opinion—to acquiesce in idealistic, cultural explanations of differences in social development, and too ready to look for unique cultural ingredients in a supposedly unique European track of development. On the other hand, these faults are all avoided in one book inspired by Weber, Randall Collins's admirable work on long-term developmental processes published under the title *Weberian Sociological Theory* (1986).

Weber and his generation did at least regard questions of long-term social development as central to history and sociology. In contrast, the three decades after the Second World War saw a "retreat of sociologists into the present."[3] This tendency may in part be the outcome of the sociology profession's wish to measure its achievements against the utilitarian yardstick of usefulness in rectifying the ills of contemporary society. It may also be in part a reflection of intellectual influences such as those of anthropology and of philosophers of science—Sir Karl Popper notable among them. In a book one purpose of which is to advocate the study of long-term processes, this deserves some comment.[4]

The rise within anthropology after the First World War of the approach known as "functionalism," associated especially with Bronislaw Malinowski and A.R. Radcliffe-Brown, had a strong but markedly delayed impact on sociology. Functionalism involved studying societies as systems of well-meshing "parts" at a given point in time.[5] It was at its peak in sociology during the two decades after the Second World War when Talcott Parsons—who had spent a year at the London School of Economics under Malinowski in the 1920s—dominated American sociology, and American sociology dominated the world. In anthropology, functionalism had begun as a methodological rule of thumb in fieldwork: it was a reaction against the tendency of Victorian evolutionary anthropologists to resort to "conjectural history" in seeking to explain the customs of preliterate societies, when for the most part any firm evidence about the past of such societies was lacking. Seeking synchronic relationships between patterns which could actually be observed in the field made better sense for anthropologists than speculating about their origins in past time. Why the same ahistorical approach should have had such appeal to sociologists studying societies blessed with abundant written records of their own past development gives more pause for thought.

By the late 1960s, functionalism was in retreat in sociology across the world. The "developmental agnosticism" (Wittfogel's phrase) it had helped sustain, however, was then strengthened once more through the influence of French structuralism on anthropologists and a minority of sociologists. Inspired by the shift in linguistics since Saussure from diachronic to synchronic investigations, Claude Lévi-Strauss sought the supposed eternal unchanging properties of the human mind underneath the surface flux and diversity. And in the hands of Lévi-Strauss and Roland Barthes, all history became myth.

Last of the culprits: Sir Karl Popper. Whether he had a powerful independent influence, or whether his views simply resonated with the currents just described, is an open question. At any rate, his books *The Open Society and Its Enemies* (1945) and *The Poverty of Historicism* (1957) had, in Britain and perhaps elsewhere, a great impact on sociologists. Whatever may have been Popper's actual intention, my own generation of undergraduates in the mid-1960s somehow picked up the idea that it was academically and politically suspect to explain the present characteristics of society by any reference to the past.[6]

While sociologists and anthropologists were abandoning history, something similar was happening among historians. Historians, needless to say, could hardly abandon history. But there was a shortening of time spans. Perhaps it was increasing professionalization of the discipline that propelled a retreat to the respectability of studies of short periods—at most, textbooks on one century or so, with a rare daring excursus to such stretches as the long sixteenth century (1500-1640).

Times have changed. Long-term social processes are once more under investigation by historians and social scientists. This is certainly not a single unified movement. Several new and unrelated tributaries seem to be flowing together, but the rediscovery of the past by social scientists and of the very long-term by historians is at least as difficult to explain as the previous retreat. In part it is just a coincidence of key individuals.[7] They were often responding to a clear lack of historical context provided in recent work in their own very varied fields. Among sociologists, *Passages from Antiquity to Feudalism* and *Lineages of the Absolutist State* by the Marxist historian Perry Anderson (1974a, 1974b) were widely read, and so have been the three volumes to date of Immanuel Wallerstein's *The Modern World-System* (1974, 1980, 1989). John A. Hall (1985), Michael Mann (1986, 1993), and Ernest Gellner (1988) have also made notable forays into world history, the renewed respectability of which among sociologists was marked by Wallerstein's election in 1994 as president of the International Sociological Association. Goudsblom and I, however, have for many years been working under the influence of someone whose at times lonely stand for a broad developmental sociology dates back more than half a century, and whose work only received wider recognition in the 1970s and 1980s: Norbert Elias. His influence will be clear in our contributions to this book, and especially in my concluding chapters 6 and 7, where I explore first the relationship between civilizing and *de*civilizing processes, and then the possibilities and difficulties of discerning in the history of Asia processes comparable to the European civilizing process depicted by Elias (1994). All three of us have also long held in high esteem the work of William H. McNeill who, although honored as a president of the American Historical Association for books of great historical sweep like *The Rise of the West* (1963), *Plagues and Peoples* (1976), and *The Pursuit of Power* (1982), remains to some extent a liminal figure who has said that his work is not yet regarded as quite respectable by the majority of his fellow historians. In the background too there has been the enormously influential work of the Annales school, the dominant voice for a generation and more among French historians. They, certainly, stressed the *longue durée*, although their work—inspiring as it is—in my opinion does relatively little to advance our *theoretical* understanding of long-term processes.[8]

Within the discipline of history, the rediscovery of the very long-term may in part have been linked to the return of the survey course in undergraduate history teaching (Jones 1985). In the 1980s, there was increasing recognition of the problems posed by the fragmentation of syllabuses, especially evident in the United States where a loss of nerve following the Vietnam War appears to have led to the abandonment of old-style "Western Civilization" courses. The volume edited by Josef W. Konvitz (1985) documents the debate about whether students should be taught resuscitated "Western Civilization" or newer "World History" courses. Whatever the outcome, and especially in view of the deterioration of secondary education almost everywhere, it is not surprising that the need was first felt in lesser institutions where the caliber of students was such that they could not be trusted to have acquired or to "get up" a standard acquaintance with the prevailing historical and cultural reference points. The need was less obvious at the Oxfords and Harvards—though in fact Oxford has instituted a comparative history course. The new world history movement is, however, far from merely undergraduate-centered, as is shown by the establishment of the new *Journal of World History* from 1990.

Within anthropology, there are also some signs of change. The controversial Marvin Harris has long pursued what he thinks of as a "materialist" view, but which in our opinion would better be called an evolutionary and ecological perspective, implicitly developmental in its mode of explanation. More recent symptoms of a revival of evolutionary theory among anthropologists are the books by C.R. Hallpike (*The Principles of Social Evolution,* 1986) and Tim Ingold (*Evolution and Social Life*, 1986). Ingold writes:

> By and large, recent anthropology has turned its back on evolution for all the wrong reasons. Of these, the most commonly cited is the one that equates the evolutionary paradigm with the establishment of a rank-order of societies that invariably places ourselves at the top. That is not, however, an essential aspect of the paradigm; what *is* essential to it is the idea that all human groups (ourselves included) are fellow passengers in the same overall movement, one that is irreversible and progressive, and hence that the differences between them must be relative to where they stand in it. But relativist anthropology, rejecting the notion of evolutionary progress and substituting the many worlds of culture for the one human world, in fact turned the imputed superiority of ourselves over others, observers over observed, into an *absolute* one. The enlightened few, liberated from the illusions of ethnocentrism with which all others were supposed to be afflicted as a condition of their belonging to one culture or another, could claim complete emancipation from the humdrum existence of ordinary people. (Ingold 1986, xii-xiii)

The differences between the biological and social realms are such that we ourselves prefer to speak of social "development," not social evolution.[9] Nevertheless, carefully used, ideas of adaptation and selection have a part to play in explaining social and economic development, as all our contributions to this book show. This, however, cuts little ice in the anthropological world, where the dominant voice is the intensely idealistic, relativist, and *un*developmental "symbolic" anthropology led especially by Clifford Geertz,[10] who has also had a powerful influence on the school of "ethno-historians."[11]

Eric Jones's theoretical roots lie in economics. Of all the social sciences, economics is the most committed to explanations in terms of timeless, eternal laws of human motion, illustrated for the most part by reference to contemporary data. Jones, however, specialized for some years in the economic history of agriculture—and the pace of agricultural change through history is particularly conducive to taking the perspective of the *longue durée*. He describes his present theoretical position as "a modified, ecological, economist's approach." He shares some of the concerns of the "New Institutional Economics" (see Basu et al. 1987). One of its principal endeavors has been described as the "endogenization of institutions"; that is to say, the aim is to bring institutions—the structural organization of societies—inside economic theories instead of leaving them outside as merely "givens." Of course, propositions about the structure of institutions have always been an essential component of economic theory. To give one simple example, Keynes's discussion of savings and investment involves propositions not only about rational choice (decisions to save and to invest) but also about institutional structure (that the two kinds of decisions are taken at any one time by two institutionally segregated categories of people). What economics has not done, on the whole, is to endogenize institutional *change*.

Finally, a little about the origins of this book. During Michaelmas term 1988, the three of us jointly conducted a seminar on "Very Long-Term Economic and Social Processes" at the University of Exeter. Johan Goudsblom had independently discovered Eric Jones's work through reading *The European Miracle* some years earlier. I eventually effected an introduction between the two of them, and then the opportunity arose for us to explore our common interests when both Goudsblom and Jones were in Exeter at the same time, Goudsblom's appointment as visiting professor of sociology overlapping with one of Jones's periods visiting from La Trobe University as professor of economic history. Our papers achieved limited circulation when issued, under the title *Human History and Social Process,* by the University of Exeter Press in 1989. For the present version, not only the title of the book is new. All the chapters have been revised and updated, and my original concluding chapter has been replaced by two different ones, based on later essays. I should like to acknowledge the support of the Australian Research Council for the research of which chapter 7 is an early product, and also to thank my research assistant at Monash, Mary Quilty. All three of us would once again like to thank the members of the original Exeter seminar—particularly Jonathan Barry, Stephen Fisher, Ian Hampsher-Monk, Michael Havinden, Helen Hintjens, Joe Melling, and Nadira Yakir—and, visiting from Oxford and Leicester respectively, John H. Goldthorpe and Eric Dunning.

Notes

1. For a full discussion of Norbert Elias's notion of "process theories" and their place in his theory of knowledge, see Mennell (1989a, 176–81, 252–58, 274–75n). As Goudsblom implies in a note to chapter 1 below, William McNeill has independently reached a similar conception of process theories as the aim of historical research; see his book *Mythistory and Other Essays* (McNeill 1986, 43–67).

2. John L. Anderson (1991) provides an extremely useful short account and critique of the rival theories of long-term economic change.

3. The phrase is Elias's (1987b). Goudsblom (1977, 7) has coined the useful word "hodiecentrism" (by comparison with "ethnocentrism") to designate the today-centered thinking of so much modern sociology.

4. I have developed this argument at greater length in my paper "The Sociological Study of History: Institutions and Social Development" (Mennell 1989b).

5. For a discussion of "functionalism" and its relation to evolutionary theories, see Mennell (1974, 141–67).

6. For a defense of developmental sociology against the claims of Popper, see Dunning (1977). For a recent restatement of Popperian views by one of Britain's most distinguished sociologists, see John H. Goldthorpe (1991), and the debate about his article in the *British Journal of Sociology* 45 (1): 1–77 (1994).

7. See the Supplementary Bibliographical Guide in the second edition of Jones's *The European Miracle* (1987, 272–74).

8. The notion of the *longue durée* was sufficient to earn the Annales school a chapter by Stuart Clark (1985) in Quentin Skinner's collection *The Return of Grand Theory in the Social Sciences.*

9. Stephen K. Sanderson (1990) argues for what he calls "evolutionism without developmentalism." Although I entirely agree with his argument—he is pursuing a nonteleological, nonunilinear form of what I would call developmental theory—he uses the two words "evolutionism" and "developmentalism" in precisely the opposite sense to our usage. That is, I think, because Nisbet (1969) made "developmentalism" a dirty word among American sociologists, whereas in the world of British anthropology

and sociology, the same connotations have remained attached to "evolutionism." The nomenclature is confusing, but in the underlying argument there is no disagreement.

10. See Geertz (1973). Elias was especially subtle on the problem of steering between what he called the Scylla of philosophical absolutism and the Charybdis of sociological relativism; see Elias (1978, 53 ff.; 1989). See my discussion of cultural relativism and anthropological arguments against Elias's theories (Mennell 1989a, 227–41).

11. Prominent ethnohistorians include Robert Darnton (see, for example, Darnton [1984], and the critique by Roger Chartier [1985], Greg Dening [1980], and Rhys Isaac [1983].

———— Chapter 1 ————

Human History and Long-Term Social Processes: Toward a Synthesis of *Chronology* and *Phaseology*

Johan Goudsblom

The Widening Range of "Human History"

The terms in the title of this chapter stem from two different, and diverging, traditions in European culture. First there is the idea of "human history" in the sense of "history of humanity." This idea goes back as far as classical antiquity, where it culminated in St. Augustine's bold attempt in *The City of God* to combine biblical history and pagan Roman history into one ecumenical history describing the vicissitudes of humanity from its earliest beginnings to the present.

The conception of an overarching human history has continued to inspire European writers well into the modern era. When viewed from a present-day vantage point, however, most of the works produced in this tradition appear to be hampered by some severe limitations. Instead of dealing with all of humanity, they actually followed only one particular strand in the history of humankind; what they did was to put the Greco-Roman and, ever since St. Augustine, the Judeo-Christian world into a historical perspective by following an itinerary starting in Mesopotamia and leading in time through Egypt, Palestine, Greece, and Rome to Western Europe and North America (see Butterfield 1981).

Our ability to see the limitations of this trajectory is of course not simply a personal achievement. It is due to the development of human society itself, and in particular to the enormous growth of readily available knowledge, enabling us to perceive things that remained completely beyond the grasp of Herodotus and St. Augustine, or even

Voltaire and Gibbon. Our view, compared with theirs, has expanded greatly both in space and in time.

The expansion in space is obvious. As European writers in the seventeenth and eighteenth century came to realize, the inhabited world was larger than the familiar stretch from the Tigris to the Thames. Yet even for Immanuel Kant, writing toward the end of the eighteenth century, the word "humanity" still expressed primarily an ethical ideal. He could not perceive it as the obvious—and in many ways menacing—reality which it has become for us today (cf. Elias 1985, 71). Whether we like it or not, we are reminded of this reality the moment we open up a newspaper or turn on the television news. We all know that, for better or for worse, the citizens of Western Europe, the political leaders in Washington and Moscow, and the masses of the poor in Asia and Africa are mutually connected by far-reaching political, military, and economic ties which—for all of us—strongly determine not only our present way of life but our very chances of survival. Global interdependency has become a hard and undeniable fact. Along with this, the need has arisen for a "human history" that is not restricted to the old familiar trajectory but encompasses the whole world.[1]

At the same time that our idea of human history is expanding in space, it is undergoing an even more spectacular expansion in time. There is increasing evidence that the human past reaches back much further than could have been known until fairly recently. The "classical" time perspective never went beyond a span in the order of seven to ten millennia. Even as late as the eighteenth century, the most enlightened minds had no empirical evidence of human records older than the Bible and Homer. They therefore could not possibly conceive of a human history or "prehistory" extending back further than three hundred generations—whereas today every encyclopedia tells us that the human past is to be measured not in hundreds but in tens of thousands of generations.

Not only can we now be certain that there are, and have been for many millennia, human groups living in virtually every part of the world, we also have some indication of the minimum time span of human habitation in different regions of the world. Thus we know that human (or hominid) groups were already living in the Americas more than 15,000 years ago, in Australia more than 40,000 years ago, in Europe more than 700,000 years ago, in Asia more than one and a half million years ago, and in Africa more than two and a half million years ago (cf. Wenke 1984; Scarre 1988). As these figures indicate, at the same time that our vision of human history is broadening vastly in scope, we are also able to draw its outlines with greater empirical precision.

The Primacy of Chronology in History

So much for the concept of "human history." Now, before I proceed to link it to the concept of "long-term social processes," I would like to make one more remark about "history" as such.

It is fair to say that history is a means for human groups to orient themselves to their past. Clearly, for this function, as for any form of intellectual orientation, some organizing principle is necessary. The most important organizing principle for history is chronology. Chronology, according to Webster's dictionary, is "the science that deals with measuring time by regular divisions and that assigns to events their proper dates." It is, in other words, an intellectual device which helps us to arrange events in a uniform, sequential order.

Now, such a sequential order is far from being self-evident, as all of us know from experience. We are all familiar with the difficulty of establishing, when recalling different events either out of our personal pasts or of a more public nature, which of these events came first, and, no less aggravating, how long was the interval between them. In order to cope with such problems we need, as Halbwachs (1950) showed, social benchmarks; these provide the chronology we need.

The oldest surviving—albeit not altogether reliable—attempt at constructing a chronology is the famous list of Sumerian kings (Jacobsen 1939). This, and successive lists of ancient Assyrian, Babylonian, and Egyptian kings, were drawn up originally for a use different from measuring time. Their immediate purpose appears to have been to establish the legitimacy of the ruling dynasty. For all we know, they contain numerous fabrications, as do, in all likelihood, the lineage lists in the Old Testament.

In the course of time, however, the lists of kings acquired a measure of "autonomy" as instruments for charting the past. The struggle for a more "objective" chronology, one that was less subject to the ideological interests of rulers, may still be witnessed in Greek and Roman historiography, for example in Thucydides' meticulous ordering by season of events in the Peloponnesian war. In the long run, the Olympic Games in Greece, and the consulates in the Roman republic, came to serve as "objective" time grids—generally accepted means of orientation in the past, relatively independent from the rulers' claims of legitimacy (see Bickerman 1980). Still, using the names of monarchs as the markers for a chronology is a custom that persists unto the present day: we still refer to "the reign of Victoria" or "the coronation of Elizabeth II" in order to pinpoint events in time.

A characteristic feature of all chronologies (and I now deliberately use the plural) is that originally they were all inherently *place-bound*. The list of kings of one country was not fit for another—as is still the case for us today: such concepts as "Georgian" or "Edwardian" do not apply to the European continent. In fact, all periodizations which are based on a chronological ordering of events—"Middle Ages" or "Renaissance" no less than "Tokugawa" or "Meiji"—are equally place-bound. They represent attempts to characterize larger spans of time within a given chronological order that is confined in space. The continued existence of different religious calendars in the contemporary world testifies to the fact that a uniform chronology for human history at large is not something that is automatically "given."

Chronology and "Phaseology"

I now come to the second term in the title of this paper, "long-term processes." This, as far as I know, is a comparatively new concept. Its origins, however, go back to a tradition that appears to be as ancient as the idea of "history"—the tradition, that is, of conceiving of the human past not in terms of the names and dates of individuals but in terms of impersonal stages or phases.

The idea that human society went through earlier stages before it reached its present condition was first recorded around the same time as the oldest lists of kings. The most familiar form this idea took was that of the image of a progressive deterioration of human life, from a golden age through a silver age to the present miserable iron age. The Assyrians knew this wretched tale, and it emerged again both in the texts of ancient Judaism and in classical Greek literature (West 1978, 172–77).

There is a marked contrast between, let us say, the book of Numbers with its long lists of lineages, enumerating every single father and eldest son on the one hand, and Hesiod's description of the descent from the golden to the iron age on the other. Both provide orientation to the past. In the former case this is done by means of specific names, in the latter case through an evocation of general characteristics.

To take another example, think again of Thucydides' great concern with chronology, and compare it with the way Plato and Aristotle wrote about what we would now call "social evolution" or, perhaps more properly, "social development."[2] They too were referring to the past when it suited their argument, but it was a fictitious and undated past, called up only to make certain points about the present. Thus Plato began his discussion of the variety of political institutions in the third book of *The Laws* with a digression on the successive stages of shepherds, farmers, and city dwellers—a digression which was very ingeniously composed but which lacked any claim to historical accuracy or veracity. The first book of Aristotle's *Politics* contains a similar passage sketching how first the family arose, then the village, and then the city. Here too the author did not bother about historical evidence. The model served only as a stepping-stone to his theory of contemporary society in which he found the family and the village to be (rightfully) subordinate to the city.

This indeed can be said about all models of stages current in classical antiquity: they were designed primarily to explain conditions in the author's present world by showing how these had arisen out of previous conditions. The models hardly ever contained any dates or names. They were typological and indifferent to chronology and might be called "achronous." They all had a clearly evaluative tenor, as exhibited in the choice of the metals—gold, silver, and iron—to indicate the various phases. Most of the models also implied a sense of necessity. Whether the present state of affairs was decried as miserable as it was by Hesiod or appreciated positively as in Aristotle's teleological conception of the city-state, it was invariably regarded as the climax in a series of stages.

Dealing with the past in terms of stages remained an element of European culture in medieval and modern times. It became a favorite intellectual device again in the nineteenth century for the leading sociological and anthropological theorists such as Comte, Spencer, Morgan, and Tylor (cf. Harris 1968). They were all very much aware that the human past was far more extensive than conventional chronology could account for and they therefore sought to design new, general schemes of the social evolution of humanity at large. Unfortunately the available historical record was insufficient to permit them to fill in their grand schemes with empirical detail. As a result, the ironic situation arose that at a time when historians such as Ranke and Michelet were becoming increasingly concerned with establishing the exact dates of events and with demarcating periods, some of their most brilliant counterparts in sociology and anthropology were taking a cavalier attitude toward chronological precision. What mattered to them was a theory of phases which might be used not only as a means of ordering the past but also for classifying contemporary societies and institutions. Their interest, we might say, lay not so much in chronology as in "phaseology."

The word "phaseology"—which was used before by German evolutionary sociologist Müller-Lyer (1915)—may evoke derogatory associations, and not only because the mere addition of the letter "r" would turn it into a term of derision. Theories of phases, as developed in the nineteenth century, have come under an avalanche of criticism in the twentieth. Many of the objections raised (for example, by Popper 1957, and Nisbet 1969) pertain to the entire tradition of constructing phase models, from Plato and Aristotle to Marx and Spencer. Again and again, it has been remonstrated that the theories stemming from this tradition suffer from at least three serious defects: (1) they lack historic specificity and, consequently, testability; (2) they tend to mix factual and normative statements; (3) they imply a notion of inevitability and teleology. To these strictures may be added two others that have come very much to the fore in the last few decades: (4) they fail to explain the passage from one stage to the next, and (5) they are predicated upon the development of Western Europe and North America, and for this reason they are to be dismissed as "Eurocentric."

Against this total rejection of stage models I would argue that, as means of orientation, chronology and phaseology both have advantages as well as disadvantages. All a chronological sequence tells us is that one thing came *after* the other; a succession of phases has the advantage of suggesting other relationships as well, and it therefore offers the possibility of an explanation. Herein lie both the strength and the weakness of phaseology; for the relationships which a model of stages suggests may sound very promising but on closer inspection prove to be either too vague to be testable or altogether spurious.

Another possible advantage of phase models is that they need not be inherently place-bound. Whereas each historical chronology was originally wedded to a specific dynastic or imperial center, the postulated schemes of successive stages were formulated in a way that was as indifferent to place as it was to time, and this made them, at least in principle, ecumenical. The terms in which they were couched were intended to be applicable to humanity at large. But then again, this very universality often made them unamenable to ready empirical testing.

The objections raised against the evaluative tenor and the notion of inevitability inherent in stage theories may be leveled against a great deal of nineteenth-century chronological historiography as well, concerned as it was with telling the stories of nations in terms of destiny and success. Nevertheless, these features of theories of social evolution were singled out for sharp criticism by such writers as Karl Popper and Robert Nisbet, who continued to recognize the spirit of Plato in virtually every attempt at discovering stages of social development.

What these critics have failed to acknowledge is that theories about social change themselves have changed, so that the objections leveled against Plato and Aristotle or even against Comte and Tylor need no longer pertain to them. One of the changes that has occurred is a shift in emphasis from "phases" to "processes." This shift may also help to meet the objections that stage theories fail to explain the actual transition between stages and that they are implicitly "Eurocentric."

Stages Within Processes: Elementary Sequential Models

The concept of "processes" may serve as an elaboration on that of "phases" or "stages." It refers to sequences of changes in the course of which something is transformed from one phase into the next. At first sight, there appears to be a fundamental difference between processes and phases: the former seem to be dynamic—characterized by movement—whereas the latter seem to be static. At closer range, however, it is clear that processes of transformation seldom stop at a particular juncture; the normal course, certainly for social processes, is to continue in one form and direction or another, even when a new "stage" has been reached. Every stage, or phase, is a passage in an ongoing movement; it consists of minor processes and it forms a part of larger processes.

Viewed in this light, process turns out to be a more encompassing concept than stage or phase. This observation may lead to a reversal of the customary priorities in phaseology: the processes come into the foreground, with phases or stages no longer defined as stationary states but in terms of the very processes of which they are a part and through which they are generated.[3]

Stages or phases are, then, continuing episodes in an ongoing process which are characterized by some relatively lasting features. Their boundaries in time are marked by specific transitions or "turning points." In the context of human history, those turning points are of the most crucial significance which occur (1) when the process manifests itself for the very first time and (2) when (if ever) it reaches every known human society.

This may all sound highly abstract. Rather than continuing in this vein, let me give a few examples. As I have argued elsewhere, a major trend in human social evolution and history has been the increasing differentiation in way of life, and the concomitant shift in the balance of power, between human groups and all closely related animal species (Goudsblom 1990). This process of differentiation has been going on for at least two million years. It has led to a gradually increasing dominance of human groups over all other mammals. As a result, interspecific struggles between humans and other mammals have become increasingly less important for the course of human history (which is, of course, not to say that they have ceased to take place), while intraspecific struggles between human groups, especially groups organized as tribes or states, have become increasingly more important.

Within this overall trend some major catalysts may be discerned—ecological transformations, brought about by human groups, that have considerably boosted the dominance of humans over other mammals. The first of these ecological transformations was the domestication of fire. Its initial effects may have been slight, partly because of the great costs it incurred. In the long run, however, the domestication of fire has been of enormous consequence, if only because it prepared the ground for the next two transformations with which most of us are more familiar: the transition to agriculture or "agrarianization" which began three to four hundred generations ago, and the large-scale application of fossil energy or "industrialization" which gained momentum only during the last ten generations.

Now, one of the interesting points to be made about these various "sub-trends"—each of which is, of course, of momentous scope—is that they all constitute processes which are still going on. The emergence of agriculture did not put an end to the domestication of fire, nor did the Industrial Revolution put an end to agriculture. Humanity entered a new stage once certain groups began to live off cultivated plants and livestock, but it has continued to control fire and, more than that, to extend that control to a greater extent so that today temperatures of well over a hundred million degrees centigrade can be produced. A conventional classification of societies into types marked by phases, say of "agrarian" and "industrial" societies, would fail to do justice to the fundamental fact that the processes which characterized an earlier phase usually continue to operate in the consecutive phase. They may become less dominant, but they do not come to a stop.

Clearly, this processual perspective does not exclude the possibility of distinguishing phases in social development. Thus, if we take as benchmarks the three major ecological transformations brought about by humanity, we may perceive four successive stages:

1. a stage when there were no societies with control over either fire, or agriculture, or mechanical industry, or x;
2. a stage when there were at least some societies with control over fire, but none with either agriculture or mechanical industry or x;
3. a stage when there were at least some societies with control over both fire and agriculture, but none with control over fire as well as agriculture, but none with mechanical industry or x;
4. a stage when there were at least some societies with control over fire as well as agriculture and mechanical industry, but none with x.

This simple four-stage model may help us, first of all, to connect "chronology" and "phaseology." Each of the turning points marking the transition from one stage to the next can, in principle, be located in time. Even if, at present, the actual dating may still be uncertain and controversial, the issue as such is clear and open to empirical tests. In addition, the model enables us to place the development of particular societies in the context of the social development of humanity at large. Classifying a particular society as "foraging" or "agrarian" is not enough; for an understanding of any specific foraging society we need to know first of all whether it was living in stage 1, 2, or 3—that is, whether it coexisted with agrarian and industrial societies. Finally, the model may remind us that we are dealing with continuing processes; one look at it may suffice to show that the rise of mechanical industry need not have been the last ecological transformation brought about by humanity. That is why I have added the x: we may well expect to enter—or perhaps we have already entered—a fifth stage, without yet being able to identify the latest transition as clearly as the preceding ones.

There is another set of propositions that may be inferred directly from the observation of the major ecological transformations. These propositions run along the following lines:

1. there was a time when there were only groups without control over fire;
2. then there was a time when there were both groups with and groups without fire;
3. we have now reached a time when there are only groups with fire.

These statements, implying a simple three-stage model, raise fascinating problems. How was the intermediate stage reached? When and where did this happen? How long did the intermediate stage last? Why did it end and lead to phase 3, the climax stage?

With regard to control over fire, we have no empirical evidence about surviving groups representing phases 1 and 2; the discussion therefore has to remain somewhat hypothetical. With agriculture and mechanical industry we find ourselves on more solid ground, and there the same triad of propositions can be made: first, there was a phase in which no human groups had agriculture; then, one in which some groups did and others did not; and now, we have entered a phase in which every group has at least products of agriculture.

The same formulations can be made to apply to a variety of other institutions, such as writing, money, cities, or metallurgy. In each case the same sequential order can be observed, suggesting the same problems of when, where, and how (or why) the intermediate stage was first reached, and of when, where, and how it came to an end. In addition, our attention is drawn toward negative cases, where the intermediate stage did not lead to a climax stage in which the institution became universal; slavery could be an example.

The Interplay of Control and Dependency

By highlighting the three ecological transformations as major turning points in sociocultural evolution, I do not mean to imply that they are to be considered as the main "determinants" or "causes" of this evolution. They are best understood, I think, as catalysts which have triggered other processes, such as population growth and migrations, which in turn have influenced the ecological conditions with which people had to cope. In the configuration of all these continuously interlocking processes, one general principle of socio-ecological dynamics seems to be of particular significance: the interplay of increases in control and dependency.

The three ecological transformations all constitute processes in which initially "wild" natural forces are "tamed" and "domesticated," or, in other words, incorporated into human society. The "taming" implies an increase in control: the natural forces are to a certain extent subordinated to human intentions. However, in contrast to what a superficial logic might lead us to expect, "control" and "dependency" are not opposites, and increased control does not automatically entail decreased dependence. To the contrary, by adjusting their way of life—including their pattern of reproduction—to a newly attained level of "control" (over fire, over plants and animals, over fossil fuel), people make themselves increasingly dependent on that which they are controlling and on the apparatus by means of which they exert their control.

The principle of paired increases in control and dependency clearly applies to the domestication of fire. The control over fire enabled human groups to extend their food range and to enter new territories, and it made their lives in a number of ways more secure and comfortable. At the same time, however, as people grew accustomed to these advantages, it became increasingly difficult for them to do without them.

With the rise of agriculture the principle manifested itself even more compellingly. Increased control of crops led to increases in food and more often than not these resulted in increased numbers of people. In order to feed all these people, more food was needed. This led to the clearing of new land, which inevitably reduced the wild country available for gathering and hunting, so that people increasingly came to depend upon agriculture as their sole means of subsistence.

The interweaving of control and dependency—a relationship which is too subtle to be expressed in terms of one-sided causation—is a feature which may be observed in virtually all long-term social processes, and which may help to explain why these processes tend to move in a "blind" and "unplanned" way. In most cases the increases in control are likely to be the outcome of deliberate intentions, but the increases in dependency which they entail are just as likely to have been unintended and unplanned.

The principle of paired increases in control and dependency, with its implications for the blind course of social evolution, is a principle of far-reaching scope. It is not, however, a "law" which could be expressed in a fixed formula. I would rather adapt Herbert Blumer's (1969, 140–52) term "sensitizing concept," and refer to this principle as a "sensitizing idea," directing our attention toward an important feature of very long-term social processes that can be observed in a great variety of empirical instances. I would even venture the hypothesis that it is a principle of such wide scope that, unless clear instances be found in which its presence cannot be demonstrated, it may be regarded as universal.

Dominant Trends

In dealing with long-term processes it seems useful to distinguish between universal and dominant trends. The trend toward specialization, for example, may be universal, but then so may be the trend toward *de*specialization, as a part of the tendency toward social entropy that seems to be present in every society. It may not be a bad rule of thumb and not an unsound research strategy to assume that for any given trend a countertrend may be found, operating in the opposite direction. The principle of paired increases in control and dependency would support this assumption, and so would the consideration that changes which are beneficial to some people are almost bound to be harmful to others. Even if those others are small in numbers or weak in power, they are nevertheless likely to put up some resistance and this resistance then constitutes a countervailing tendency.

There would have been no sociocultural evolution, however, if every trend had always been offset by an equally strong countertrend. The problem is, therefore, to identify the dominant trends and to seek out how they may be explained.

One major trend in human history, to which I have already alluded, is the increasing differentiation in behavior and power between human groups and all other mammals. This trend has been dominant for at least two million years and it is still continuing. There can be no doubt that the long-established predominance of humans over other animals was a precondition for the emergence of agriculture around ten thousand years ago. But then, as so often happens with preconditions, this predominance was reinforced by the further development of farming.

Ever since then, over the past ten thousand years, a cluster of closely interrelated trends has been dominant in human history. They did not immediately prevail everywhere, but once set into motion in certain areas, they tended to spread until, in the twentieth century, they have become dominant trends in all societies all over the world. Maybe some societies have now reached a stage in which some of these trends are beginning to be outweighed by countervailing movements. In the large majority of contemporary societies, however, these are still the dominant trends.

As a direct result of agriculture, there was a trend toward higher production of food in increasingly more concentrated areas (from "shifting cultivation" to "multi-cropping"—see Boserup 1965, 15–16) leading to an *increase in numbers* of the human population and to an increasing *concentration* of people in ever more densely populated areas. Both within and among these areas of dense settlement there were processes of *specialization* as to social functions and of *organization* in increasingly large units such as states, markets, and religious cults. As specialization and organization proceeded, they gave rise to increasing differences in power, property, and prestige; in other words, to a process of social *stratification*.

In a way, these five trends represent variations on the theme of differentiation and integration which Herbert Spencer (1862) indicated as the twin motive forces underlying evolution in general. The growth, concentration, and increasing organization of human populations may be seen as reflecting integration, specialization as reflecting differentiation, and organization as reflecting both. In view of the close interrelations among the five trends, it would seem futile to try to identify one of them as the "prime mover." It is more fruitful to chart the course which the trends have actually taken and then to seek an explanation for their overall dynamics, including oscillations, stagnations, and regressions.

It is not difficult to think of various cases in which the trends never were dominant or ceased to be so. The "decline and fall of the Roman empire" probably comes to mind first of all, but it is by no means the only counterexample (Tainter 1988). However, even if the historical cases of stagnation and reversal turn out to outnumber those in which the five trends did proceed, the remarkable fact remains that *in the long run,* the dominant trends continued and left no society unaffected.

The "long run" is crucial. Clearly no single society has continued to veer unwaveringly through the ages in the direction of the five trends. The trends have remained dominant, however, for humanity at large. Taking the calculations of Rein Taagepera (1978) about the size and duration of empires as a clue, we could formulate the following hypotheses. Over the past ten millennia, in any random year (1) the total size of the human population and (2) the size of the then-largest concentration of people on earth has been greater than either was a thousand years before. Moreover, the highest degree of (3) specialization, (4) organization, and (5) stratification to be found anywhere in the world was also greater than it was a thousand years before. Perhaps, because we are still lacking sufficient empirical evidence and appropriate means of operationalization, these hypotheses are too bold to be testable yet. They may help, nevertheless, to make us familiar with the idea that sensible propositions about very long-term processes can be made.

Once we are prepared to accept this idea, there is no longer any reason to espouse what Karl Wittfogel (1957, 7) has aptly called "developmental agnosticism." Such agnosticism is quite rampant among historians and social scientists today. In order to overcome it, we shall have to avoid conceiving of very long-term processes in monocausal, teleological, and normative terms. The fact that social evolution has gone on in a certain direction for many millennia does not imply that it is determined by any particular cause, nor that it is attuned to any particular purpose, nor that it corresponds to any particular ideal. In each of these respects agnosticism is called for, but this skeptical attitude need not affect the conception of long-term social processes and of social development as such.

The many diverse forms which human culture can take may easily blind us to the common pattern in the processes of social development. Part of this pattern may be due to general tendencies inherent in each and every society at a certain stage of development. In addition, we shall always have to reckon with the possibility that any particular society may, because of its specific ecological and sociological conditions, initiate processes which then radiate into other, neighboring societies and acquire a momentum of their own. Population growth may be a case in point. It did not take place always and everywhere, and certainly not at the same rate (cf. Harris and Ross 1987). Even for humanity at large, growth probably did not proceed in an unbroken fashion: there were periods of stagnation and decline. In the long run the growth trend proved to be dominant, however, because societies which happened to develop high growth rates could not fail to influence those with low growth rates (and vice versa, it should be added). Changing population pressures led to waves of migration—sometimes peaceful, more often violent—which tended to follow two contrary currents: one from the centers of urban settlement to the rural areas and the periphery, and one in the opposite direction. Many of the major events in the history of individual peoples and nations have taken place, as William McNeill (1984) shows, in the context of these far-reaching migration movements.

Human History and Sociology

As I pointed out at the beginning of this chapter, there are two reasons for some of us today to engage in the study of human history, in spite of its formidable scope. One is the topicality of the subject now that humanity's increasing global interdependence is so clearly manifest. The other is the growing insight that global interdependence is far less recent than we may have been led to believe. There never was a time when the history of any people could evolve for generations without its being affected by its neighbors—who were affected by *their* neighbors, and so on. Therefore, the history of humanity forms the all-encompassing framework in which all the events have taken place that form the subject matter of more particular histories. It goes without saying that our conception of human history must be compatible with all the known facts, but it should be equally obvious that all knowledge of facts relating to specific historical events remains somewhat loose and "up in the air" if it cannot be connected with this larger framework.

As McNeill (1986, 44) remarks, "Only by accepting and then acting on a theory of social process can historians expect to have a criterion of relevance to guide them amidst the confusing plethora of data potentially available to their researches." Sociologists, on the other hand, as Michael Mann (1986, 173) notes, in drawing up their theoretical schemes and comparative models, "must be restrained by an appreciation of world-historical time." It is in the study of human history and long-term social processes that these desiderata can be jointly met: here historians attain their highest level of generality, while sociologists are confronted with the dictates of chronology. Here, more than anywhere else, it becomes evident that—as Norman Gottwald reminds us—"history without sociology is blind, sociology without history is empty" (1979, 17).

History and sociology are so complementary at this level that ideally speaking they could merge completely. In actual practice the chances for this to happen are very slight. This is largely due to the diverging group cultures which have developed historically and constitute an unavoidable social fact (cf. Burke 1992). The very lack of a synthesis in the form of a common theory of human history and social evolution reflects the professional frictions which beset the working relationships between the two disciplines. At the same time, as so often in social and cultural processes, the "effect" also operates as a "cause": the lack of a common theory continues to keep historians and sociologists apart.

Still, we should not give up our attempts to reach at least a common theoretical perspective. Such a project requires high ambitions as to its aim and range as well as modesty regarding the prospects of its realization in the near future. We certainly should not let our expectations run too high. Theories, after all, are no more than didactic models: summaries of the present state of knowledge, aimed primarily at transmitting the general principles as efficiently as possible (cf. Kuhn 1970). Only by keeping our theoretical perspective flexible and open can this task be performed. We must not strive toward a closed system designed, like Ronald Reagan's chimera of an impenetrable SDI-shield, to intercept any problem. But neither are we empty-handed, even at this date and stage.

Notes

1. See McNeill (1986). I prefer the term "human history" over "world history," since the latter, strictly speaking, refers to the history of the world as a geological process. This may, however, reflect a hypersensitivity to the literal meaning of words of someone who is not a native English speaker.

2. Cf. Elias (1991); see also Hallpike (1986) for a clear distinction between social and biological evolution.

3. Cf. Elias 1977; see also McNeill's essay, "The Rise of the West as a Long-Term Process" (1986) 43–67.

—————— Chapter 2 ——————

Ecological Regimes and the Rise of Organized Religion

Johan Goudsblom

This chapter and the following one, on "Military–Agrarian Regimes," belong together. They both deal, in a highly general way, with the origins of contemporary institutions—of organized religion and war, and the social hierarchies associated with these institutions.

I have tried to follow a consistently "processual" approach as outlined in chapter 1 and to see how this may be applied to the emergence of ruling classes of priests and warriors in agrarian societies. As the scope of my survey is very large, what I have to say is exploratory rather than conclusive. This is a personal inquiry, not a summary of "the state of the art." Its purpose is to bring together pieces of information gathered from various fields and to see how they may be fitted into a coherent perspective. As my guiding principle I have used the idea that nothing is ever self-evident and there is always room for inquiring into how things have become what they now are.[1]

Religion and Social Process

In the case of religion, this principle is incompatible with the widespread belief that religions may change but religion as such is eternal. In anthropology, this belief found expression more than a hundred years ago in Edward Tylor's (1871) theory of stages, according to which mankind, since its earliest origins, had passed through successive stages of religious evolution—from animism through polytheism to monotheism. Religion became as it were increasingly more "civilized"; but "man" was religious from the start: *Homo religiosus* appeared to be ageless.[2]

Along the same lines it could be argued that "man" is belligerent by nature; that there is an equally timeless *Homo bellicosus,* and that war, like religion, is inherent in the human condition.

In this and the following paper, I shall allow myself the freedom to doubt these postulates and, instead, to entertain the hypothesis that religion and war have been the result of particular sociocultural processes in human history. We have words in our languages such as "secularization" and "pacification" which point to movements in the opposite direction: away from religion and war. Is it not equally possible that these counter-movements were preceded by trends *toward* religion and war—by "religification" and "martialization" or "bellification"?

I shall not advocate that we enrich our vocabulary with these nasty neologisms. I only mention them in order to suggest that neither a state of war nor a state of religion need be the "natural" state for human beings to be in.

My research on the domestication of fire has only strengthened my distrust of regarding any social institution as eternal and universal.[3] The domestication of fire is a process which has been going on for hundreds of thousands of years. Studying it has imbued me with a sense of the enormous continuity of human culture: human groups have transmitted the skill of keeping a fire for many thousands of generations. Nevertheless, there *was* a time when human groups did not have fire. So, while there is impressive continuity, this does not imply timelessness.

Similarly, the social institutions and mental attitudes which we nowadays associate with "religion" may also be less universal and less ancient than we are generally taught to assume. As I shall try to show, a strong case can be made for the hypothesis that these institutions and attitudes first took shape only some 300 to 500 generations ago, after the emergence of agriculture.

Religion and the Rise of Agriculture

As I argued in chapter 1, wherever the process of agrarianization gained momentum, a cluster of five closely interrelated trends tended to become dominant:

1. toward an increase in food, and an increase in people;
2. toward greater concentrations of food, and greater concentrations of people;

3. toward an increasing specialization in the production and consumption of food, and an increasing specialization of people;

4. toward the growth of organizations allocating greater quantities of food and coordinating larger numbers of people over longer distances;

5. toward an increasing differentiation of power or "stratification" among people.

Of most interest to us at present are the third and the fifth trend, specialization and stratification. We can observe that wherever the size and density of population increased, people also became increasingly differentiated according to their occupation and, concomitantly, their rank, class, or caste. Generally speaking, four major categories emerged: peasants, artisans, priests, and warriors.

This is, of course, a very rough classification. The distinctions are not always perfectly clear and many overlapping cases may be discerned: peasants who were also artisans, artisans who were also priests, and so on. Charting all the historical varieties, however, is not my concern here. I maintain that, by and large, the fourfold classification is valid and can be applied to a great number of empirical cases.

The question then arises of how this general pattern is to be explained. It is not difficult to account for the fact that the bulk of the population consisted of peasants working the land; nor do we need to stretch our imagination to understand the emergence of craftsmen and traders. The matter becomes intriguing, however, when we turn to the formation of special classes of priests and warriors, and their rise to social dominance. In this chapter I shall focus upon the priests. The problem is, then, how in societies composed of farmers or peasants (who themselves stemmed from foragers, from gatherers and hunters) a new group of specialists, the priests, could emerge—the upper crust of which subsequently could establish itself (along with, and in rivalry with, warrior elites) as a ruling class for many centuries.[4]

Such a fundamental change as the formation of a "new class" can only be explained by relating it to other changes. It makes no sense to try to infer the rise to power of either priests or warriors from an unchanging image of "man" as a creature that has been always by nature religious and belligerent, a *Homo religiosus* and a *Homo bellicosus*. Obviously, if "man" were incapable of religion and war, neither priests nor warriors would ever have come upon the stage. But then the same could be said about space travel and so many other things.

Emphasizing process and change does not mean, however, that I wish to deny continuity. There is a great deal of continuity between pre-agrarian and agrarian societies: the control of fire, which has been an essential precondition for agriculture, is a case in point. It represents a socially acquired skill—an element of culture in the sense of being "learned, shared, and transmitted"[5]—that has been handed down from generation to generation since the Lower Paleolithic. Then, in the Upper Paleolithic, "broad spectrum economies" developed which in their highly advanced techniques of hunting and gathering as well as of storing and preserving food already anticipated pastoralism and agriculture in many ways (see Wenke 1984, 155–69).

In spite of the strong underlying continuities, the emergence of agrarian societies, using domesticated plants and animals, heralded a new stage in human social evolution and history. And it was in these agrarian societies that priests gradually came into their own as a separate and distinct class, with their specific modes of dress, habits, and professional secrets. In the European Middle Ages, the clergy adorned itself with the title "First Estate." This may not any longer have reflected the actual power relations; but it did correspond with the fact that, from a historical point of view, the priests probably *were* the First Estate. If we can speak of an "oldest profession," it may well be that of priesthood.[6] (Incidentally, the very word that we still use to indicate a ranking order of established authority is "hierarchy"—which literally means "holy rule," "rule by priests.")

It may even be due to the long-standing influence of priests that the problem of the social origins—the sociogenesis—of the office and authority of priests is seldom raised. After all, viewed from a priestly tradition itself, this question is pointless, for the institution of priesthood as a First Estate or highest caste is regarded as a divine and timeless arrangement which does not need to be explained in sociological or sociogenetic terms at all.

The Persistence of Theological Reasoning

Interestingly, this theological train of thought still resounds in most scholarly writing about religion and priests today—even by authors who would not hesitate to regard their own approach as thoroughly secular. It is quite common to say that the priests fulfill a "mediating role" between human beings and "the spirit world" or "the supernatural" or "the gods." I could fill the rest of this paper with quotations illustrating this way of writing about priests.[7] I shall restrict myself to a small selection from a book on the doctrine of the three orders or three estates in medieval Europe by the French historian Georges Duby. "The bishop," he writes, "was a sacred personage, a Christ, the Lord's Anointed; passing through his skin, mixing with, penetrating his entire body, the chrism impregnated him forever with divine power." . . . "Anointment," Duby continues, "brought with it another gift: *sapientia*, a gaze capable of penetrating behind the veil of appearances to reach hidden truths. Only the bishop possessed the keys to the truth." Or, in other words, "Anointment had placed the bishop right at the point where heaven and earth were joined, between the visible and the invisible. . . . Because of his median, intermediary position, the bishop bore a special obligation to contribute to the harmony between the two worlds, that essential concord which Satan strove ceaselessly to disrupt" (Duby 1980, 14–15).

Clearly, these words carry a theological ring. Anthropologists might say that Duby is giving an "emic" description: he puts himself into the frame of mind of the medieval bishops themselves to such an extent that he is actually only paraphrasing the doctrine they propounded *in their own terms;* until, rather suddenly, he switches to an "etic" idiom, as he concludes: "In the Carolingian tradition, the episcopate was by nature the producer of ideology" (1980, 16).

I must admit that I find all this somewhat unsatisfactory and, frankly speaking, a bit too easy. If we take Duby literally, there was a god, there were people, laymen, and the bishop's authority rested on the fact that he mediated between these two parties. Or maybe we should interpret Duby's words more liberally, as if he is actually saying: "There was a religion, a belief, and according to this belief the bishop played a mediating role." But even then the question remains why all the other people were willing to accept a set of beliefs that was so obviously to the bishop's advantage.

Again, instead of Duby I could have chosen many other examples. This is the customary way in which historians, anthropologists, and sociologists write about religion and priests. One other example can serve as a stepping-stone to my further argument. It is a description of temple ceremonies in ancient Mesopotamia by the archaeologist Seton Lloyd, whose expert knowledge I do not doubt for a moment. But note the words he has chosen:

> High amongst the services which the gods required of their worshippers was the provision of food, drink, and oil for anointing. According to H.W.F. Saggs "The gods enjoyed regular meals . . . which were deposited upon tables before the divine images." Their food included bread in large quantities, the meat of sheep or cattle and drink in the form of beer, which was greatly favoured by the Sumerians. Among provisions listed in later times were honey, ghee, fine oil, milk, dates, figs, salt, cakes, poultry, fish and vegetables.

For those who still might wonder after reading this extensive menu how it was actually consumed by the gods, the description is followed by a brief explanation in small print:

> The meal of the god was technically a banquet to which other deities [?] were invited and at which the human worshippers and even the dead [?] might be present. The gods themselves received special parts of the animals, the remainder going to the king, the priests and the temple staff. (Lloyd 1984, 44)

In the last sentence, I think, we get a glimpse of what actually went on during these temple feasts. The ceremonies were held in honor of the gods, but these gods (that is to say, their images) were only provided with "special parts" of the meat; the rest went, to repeat, "to the king, the priests, and the temple staff."

I suggest that instead of writing that the meals were served to the gods, it might be more straightforward to state that they were intended for a group of men, mainly priests.

In this respect, something might be learned from the texts of ancient Judaism, which could be surprisingly candid on this score. I am not directly referring to such anecdotes as the one in the Book of Daniel which tells us how the priests of Bel in Babylon used to let themselves secretly into the temple at night to indulge in the food that had been sacrificed at the altar during the day—a piece of gossip revealing how the adherents of different religions regarded each other's ceremonies (Daniel 14: 1–22). More interesting in our present context is the wealth of information in the opening chapters of Leviticus about the proceedings in the service of the Jewish religion itself and about the portions of various sacrifices to which the priests were entitled. Leviticus lists various types of offerings: burnt offerings, meat offerings, sin offerings, trespass offerings, consecrations, and peace offerings. Each type of sacrifice had its own rules; in some, the whole animal was burnt, as "an offering made by fire, of a sweet savor unto the Lord," whereas in others, only a few stipulated parts were burnt and the remainder was allocated to the priests. They, and they alone, should eat it, "for it is most holy"; no lay person was allowed to touch it: if anything was still left over on the third day, that "shall be burnt with fire" (Lev. 7: 5, 17).

Not all the priests of Israel appear to have been as particular about these rules. Here is what the first Book of Samuel has to say about the sons of the priest Eli who worked for their father in the temple of Shiloh:

> Now the sons of Eli were sons of Belial; they knew not the Lord. And the priests' custom with the people was, that, when any man offered sacrifice, the priest's servant came, while the flesh was in seething, with a fleshhook of three teeth in his hand. And he struck it into the pan, or kettle, or cauldron, or pot; all that the fleshhook brought up the priest took for himself. So they did in Shiloh unto all the Israelites that came thither. Also before they burnt the fat, the priest's servant came, and said to the man that sacrificed, Give flesh to roast for the priest; for he will not have sodden flesh of thee, but raw. And if any man said to him, Let them not fail to burn the fat presently, and then take as much as thy soul desireth; then he would answer him, Nay; but thou shalt give it to me now; and if not, I will take it by force. Wherefore the sin of the young men was very great before the Lord; for men abhorred the offering of the Lord. (1 Sam. 2: 12–17)

This story clearly exposes abuse of the priestly office. It also shows us something of the balance of power between the priests who controlled the altar and the ordinary people who came to it with their offerings. Apparently, the priests took in food and possibly other revenues as well; in this respect they were at the receiving end. What did they do in exchange which made the other people willing to support them?

With regard to any form of regularly recurring social behavior we may safely assume, I think, that (unless the power balance is very uneven) it fulfills certain functions for the various people involved. In the case of the sons of Eli, it is not difficult to see some of the functions the rites of sacrifice had for *them;* the intriguing question is what functions the rites had for those who came to offer their meat and their bread.

Obviously, the scope of this question is by no means restricted to ancient Israel. In a great many other agrarian societies, past and present, similar arrangements prevailed, with priests being able to support themselves through the gifts of others. What precisely was the nature of the social service they provided in return?

The Rise of Agrarian Regimes

Agrarian societies, regardless of their many varieties, have one common feature in which they differ significantly from the far more ancient type of foraging society in which people had been living for thousands of generations. They are both more productive and more vulnerable.

Agriculture involves deliberate intervention by human groups in the blind process of natural selection between and within species. It involves sustained attempts at eliminating the growth of unwanted plants from a field and fostering the growth of wanted plants—primarily those known to be edible. The effort required is known as work; the result, if successful, is increased productivity.

Note that this is a sociological way of conceiving of productivity. Economists—and many anthropologists who have dealt with this issue as well—tend to define productivity as output per man-hour.[8] This individual-centered definition leads to the conclusion that foraging societies were more productive than agrarian societies, for people did not have to work as hard. Such a conclusion is misleading, however, in that it diverts our attention from the undeniable fact that, on the whole, as collectivities, agrarian societies produced greater quantities of food than gatherers and hunters ever did.

This fact had far-reaching consequences. Because the land they worked yielded more products that were useful to them and fewer that were useless, increasing numbers of people could find subsistence in a given area. Whenever, as a result, the population increased, it grew more dependent upon the very products of agriculture. There were more mouths to be fed, while the "wild" terrain suitable for gathering and hunting diminished. Consequently, the only resources left for people were their crops and their livestock, and this state of one-sided dependency made them especially vulnerable.

Three types of danger with which people always had to cope became all the more threatening to agrarian communities. The types of danger I am referring to form a triad, corresponding to what Norbert Elias has called a "triad of basic controls" (1978, 156–57). First, there were the many dangers that came from the nonhuman, or *extrahuman,* world: droughts or, the opposite, rains and floods; parasites; weeds; exhaustion of the soil. Second, there were the dangers emanating from *interhuman* relations: the always lurking chance that hostile groups of humans would pillage and destroy the crops and the stores. And, third, there was the risk that the harvest would fail or be lost through faulty sowing, nursing, harvesting, or storing—in other words, through mismanagement due to *intrahuman* nature: to negligence, ignorance, or greed, to lack of care, discipline, or foresight.

The threefold classification of extra-, inter-, and intrahuman dangers may help us, I think, to explain the emergence of priests and warriors in agrarian societies, including the sequence in which they emerged. (The issue of sequence is only secondary, however, to my main thesis regarding the sociogenesis of priestly and warrior groups as such.)

During the first stages of agriculture the dangers of predation and plunder by other human groups were relatively small; there was not much to steal, and there were few potential robbers around. All the greater, however, were the dangers involved in the extrahuman forces of nature that could ruin a harvest, and in the intrahuman inclination toward laziness and self-indulgence that could have equally devastating effects.

Although some of us today may be inclined to view the life of farmers or peasants in preindustrial societies as standing "close to nature," cultivating crops is certainly not something inborn that is given to humanity "by nature." Everything about it has to be learned and it poses problems which can only be handled with the aid of elaborate sociocultural arrangements.

Paramount among the problems with which the early agriculturalists had to cope was, of course, the question of how to deal with the plants and animals they were trying to "domesticate." The process of domestication implied that groups of people entered into a new symbiosis with some specially favored species which they had originally encountered in the wild, which they now began to take under their own care, and which they tried to subject to an ecological regime controlled by themselves.

In order to establish this regime, people had to have knowledge of the plants and animals and of the conditions furthering or impeding their growth. They needed, in other words, knowledge of "extrahuman nature." The evidence suggests that this was an area in which priests claimed—and to some extent also possessed—expertise. When in the literature mention is made of the "mediating role" that priests fulfilled between the ordinary people and the "supernatural," the authors usually are referring to some sort of competence—real or alleged—in dealing with problems regarding the weather and the seasons, or parasites and pests.

Thus priests often took upon themselves the task of "timing." It was—and still is—of vital interest for farmers to know when the moment had come to till the land, to sow, to weed, to harvest, to break into the winter stocks. If they started sowing or planting too early, the young seedlings might freeze or be washed away by a torrent of rain; postponing the sowing too long would mean, on the other hand, that precious days of growth would be lost and weeds could sprout too easily. Harvesting raised similar problems: if done too soon, one would miss the chance of further ripening; if done too late, the crops might be exposed to rain or frost.

Human beings are not equipped with a "biogram" for agrarian life. They have no innate calendar telling them when the time is ripe for preparing the soil, for planting the seeds, for removing weeds, for harvesting. The only calendar available to people is a sociocultural one: among the tasks with which priests in agrarian societies used to be entrusted was the management of the calendar. They had to register, by observing the position of sun, moon, and stars, whether the time had come for certain agrarian activities.

Orientation was not all, however. In *Time: An Essay,* Norbert Elias quoted from the memoirs of an old Krobo man (the Krobo are a tribe living in what is now Ghana) describing how in the olden days, the priest used to determine the moment when the farmers had to go out and sow their wheat. In order to do so, he would climb the mountain at the center of the Krobo territory every morning to observe the sunrise. Once the sun made its first appearance behind a certain rock, the priest would shout a signal which resounded all over the mountain, and then "you would see the farmers and their families running down the mountain with their hoes and baskets to join or share in the labour" (Elias 1992, 50).

Even if the informant quoted by Elias may have drawn a slightly idealized picture of the ritual—which he had never witnessed himself, because it had already died out before he was a child—his description remains valuable as an account of the functions attributed to priests. Another detail is also worth noting: people were allowed to repeat the priest's signal, a magical formula, while they were sowing; but if anyone dared to do so later, after the sowing was done, he would be punished severely and he might even be sent away in slavery.

This piece of information clearly brings out that the agrarian regime was not just a regime over plants and animals but also over people.[9] As a regime over people it consisted, to use Elias's terms, in part of external constraints and in part of—complementary—self-restraints. Priests played a prominent part in it; and they were able to do so, I think, because their task was vitally important for the entire community—not only because of the orientation they provided but, perhaps even more so, because of the discipline they exerted. The discipline could be binding, even if the grounds on which the priests based their decisions appeared to be unfathomable and arbitrary. In uncertain situations a randomly given directive would at least bring the relief that someone was prepared to assume responsibility.

Again, I do not wish to suggest that the problems with which farmers had to cope were altogether new, and had never bothered gatherers and hunters. My point is that as agrarian communities grew in size and density, some problems became particularly acute and could only be met through special forms of discipline. I am thinking of the need to *work* hard in order to produce food; the need to *store* stocks of food and seed for a considerable time; and the need to *distribute* these stocks among the members of the community in a fair and satisfactory way.

In a series of thought-provoking papers and books, the anthropologist Marvin Harris (1974, 1977, 1985, 1993) has turned our attention to the fact that in agrarian communities, the problems of preserving and distributing food were no less compelling than those of producing it. In order to be able to survive periods of scarcity, these communities would have to attain a level of production exceeding their immediate needs in normal times. Such abundance might ordinarily not seem necessary in the short term, but in the longer run, as a buffer against unforeseen exigencies, it was. I would argue that rites conducted by priests helped to strengthen the self-restraint which could keep people from too readily drawing upon their reserves.

Think once more of the Old Testament, which to many of us is the most familiar source about life under a strict agrarian regime. The teachings it contains are typically directed to people who everyday found themselves confronted with the sort of problems I have just mentioned. They had to earn their bread by the sweat of their brow; they had to be thrifty; and they had to see to it that no one among their own kin suffered need—for the presence of people living in destitution could form a serious menace to a small farming community. Diligence, frugality, and a sense of social responsibility—these were the prime virtues. And admonitions to live up to them were accompanied by the endlessly repeated call to obedience to God: one always had to observe one's religious duties and do honor to the priests.

It should be clear that although I keep referring to the Bible, my argument is couched in a developmental rather than biblical train of thought. I observe that the great majority of agrarian societies in the past had priests; this leads me to the question of which (socially formed) needs the priests met or, in other words, which functions they fulfilled that could serve to explain their prominent position. I am even prepared to argue that, at a certain stage of agrarian development, societies *with* priests had greater chances of survival than societies *without* priests.

The functions of priests, in my view, included both orientation and discipline—with regard to work and production, and also with regard to problems of storing and distributing, of preservation and consumption. I particularly wish to stress that the latter problems were at least as important as those of work and production. A successful harvest brought in at a single time a far greater quantity of food than foragers could ever collect—more, too, than the best catch of the hunters of large game. This harvest would be the main subsistence for the entire community for many months to come. All this raised unprecedented problems, constituting many potential sources of uncertainty and conflict. The priests, I would argue, offered binding solutions to these problems in the form of rites. These rites, to be performed by themselves or under their direction, were standard ways of coping with the problems arising from the social conditions in which the farmers found themselves living.

As I pointed out, these problems had to do with external, extrahuman as well as with internal, intrahuman nature. For a harvest to be successful, people always remained dependent upon sun, wind, and rain—natural forces over which they could exert no control but to which they could try to adjust themselves to the best of their knowledge. What Calvinist theologians later were to say about divine grace also applied to a successful harvest: even if you did your best, you could never be sure that the outcome would be good; but if you failed to do your best, a bad outcome would certainly lie ahead of you. Priests, I think, helped to impress this insight upon people and to make them live in accordance with it, so that, for the sake of a harvest which would always remain uncertain, they would be willing to summon the patience and the industry without which the crops were bound to fail.

This was not all. Even if a rich harvest were reaped, the community had not nearly come to the end of its problems. On the contrary, it was put to the test once more. How could some—the strongest—members of the community be prevented from seizing the sudden plenitude and appropriating the best parts of it, or, worst of all, feast on it until nothing remained, neither food nor seed corn?

The problems of preservation and distribution were all the more pressing since greed tends to be contagious. If a few members of a group helped themselves too eagerly from the supplies, others could hardly afford to lag behind. Whoever failed to join in would appear to harm himself and his own. How, then, could this vicious circle be broken?

It was broken, I think, by an invention that was as simple as it was ingenious and the importance of which can hardly be overrated. A social institution was developed which offset both the individual inclination toward greed in the face of sudden abundance and the social mechanism of contagion triggered by it. The institution I have in mind was that of harvest feasts. During a brief period, the community was allowed to feast collectively on the crops; but after a few days the feast was called to an end and frugal times began again. The feasts were led by the priests. They were also the ones to terminate the feasting.

The pressures of frugality under which agriculturalists lived rested even more heavily upon those (and they were the majority) who combined agriculture with pastoralism. In addition to their stores of crops they also had, so to speak, an excellent supply of meat permanently at hand. The temptation to kill an animal in times of adversity was therefore always present. What could be more effective to counter this temptation than making slaughter into a strictly ritual activity, to be performed only by the priests or, at best, with priestly permission? Could it be purely accidental, we may well ask ourselves, that Easter happens to fall in early springtime, shortly after the tender lambs are born?

These considerations help us to understand the seemingly paradoxical fact that in the rites of harvest and slaughter not only feasting but also sacrifice played a central role. Making a sacrifice, so it seems, became the standard way in which people expressed their willingness to deny themselves certain immediately tempting pleasures, and to submit to a regime of renunciation, even in the midst of plenitude.

In an interesting historical and anthropological study, Bruce Lincoln has compared two seminomadic peoples whose primary means of subsistence was cattle: the Indo-Iranians of the third and second millennia B.C., and the Nilotics of Eastern Africa, many of whom are still leading a similar existence today. Among both peoples, slaughtering cattle was strictly forbidden, unless it was done by priests. Among the Dinka in Eastern Africa, Lincoln (1981, 44) writes, "No man will take it upon himself to kill so valuable and beloved an animal as an ox or cow simply because he is hungry"; it is only as a sacrifice that an ox may be done to death. The Indo-Iranians acted no differently: in their language one and the same word apparently stood for "domesticated animal," "cattle," and "sacrificial animal"; another word may be translated either as "cattle" or as "that which may only be killed as a sacrifice" (Lincoln 1981, 65, 155–56).

One problem remains intriguing. In the offering rituals from Mesopotamia and ancient Israel to which I referred above, the sacrifices were made up mostly of meat, and first-rate meat at that (for in these ceremonies only the best seemed good enough and only animals without blemish were accepted). As I pointed out, considerable portions of this meat were eaten by the priests. If we are to believe the book of Leviticus, however, this was not always the case. There were occasions when the entire sacrifice, which might be a splendid bull, was burnt and sent up in smoke. How could *this* apparent waste be explained sociologically? What chances of survival were enhanced by letting precious food go up into thin air?

This question, too, may perhaps be answered by putting it within the context of the problems of preservation and distribution. Again, a helpful clue may be found in the work of Marvin Harris, although he can be held in no way responsible for the hypothesis I am about to offer. A radical way to get rid of the problem of distributing food that has become chronically scarce, he writes, is simply to make this food forbidden for everybody—as has happened with pork among the Jews and the Muslims and with beef among the Hindus (Harris 1977, 193–232). Both taboos are seen by Harris as the result of a long-term historical process of intensification of agriculture leading to ecological changes which made the keeping of pigs and cows increasingly costly. As a domesticated species, pigs had little more to offer than their meat, and that could be done without. Oxen and cows, on the other hand, provided the human population of India with vitally necessary services such as traction power and milk. Whereas the most ancient Vedic scriptures gave detailed instructions on how priests were to slaughter cattle, later Hindu traditions have sanctified the cow as a sacred animal, just as in the Middle Eastern religions the pig has been declared unclean.

Letting a sacrifice go up in smoke is a way of tabooing it: this is food that no one may touch anymore, not even a priest. Could it be that this custom originated somewhat along the following lines? It would seem likely that in a society of pastoralists such as the Indo-Iranians, people occasionally tried to evade the ban on slaughtering, and it is equally likely that some of them were caught in the act. What was to happen in such a situation? The offender would have to be punished, of course, but what was to be done with the killed animal? Since it would seem highly improper to let other people feast on it, a more drastic solution seemed called for: that of ostentatiously burning the entire animal that had been wrongly killed.

Let me make one further step on this increasingly speculative track and venture the supposition that while the sacrifice was being made, the spectators at such ceremonies may have pondered to *whom* it was being made. Who might be the recipient of this delicious meat?

I do not wish to claim that the idea of gods originated exclusively in this sort of ritual; but I do think that these rituals helped to shape it. The ritualization of slaughter and its monopolization by the priests went hand in hand with what would now be called the "criminalization" of nonritual killing, eventually resulting in its virtual elimination.

The offering rituals, like the harvest feasts, were ceremonies with strong disciplinary functions. In the long run, agricultural and pastoral groups observing such rituals stood a better chance of surviving than groups resisting such rituals. The priests, who served as the masters of the ceremonies, bolstered the rituals with ideas about a world of gods who would be the grateful (if not wrathful) receivers of the delicacies which those who brought their offerings were denying themselves. In doing so, the priests also advanced the idea that they were the intermediaries between this world in which people lived and worked and the other, "supernatural" world, and that in this function, as intermediaries, they were indispensable.

I realize that I have ended on a very speculative note. Let me therefore briefly summarize the main points I have tried to make:

1. I have noted a tendency among historians, anthropologists, and sociologists to deal with problems of religion and priesthood too readily in theological terms.
2. I have then tried to state the problem of how priests came to be a ruling group in agrarian societies as a sociological problem.
3. I have tried to find a solution by applying the concept of agrarian regime, and argued that priests fulfilled important functions in agrarian regimes, providing both orientation and discipline.

Notes

1. As Gellner observes in the opening paragraphs of *Plough, Sword and Book* (1988, 11): "Men and societies frequently treat the institutions and assumptions by which they live as absolute, self-evident, and given. They may treat them as such without question, or they may endeavour to fortify them by some kind of proof. In fact, human ideas and social forms are neither static nor given."

2. On Tylor's and other late Victorian views of the development of religion, see also Harris (1968, 201–7).

3. Goudsblom (1986, 1987, 1992a, 1992b). See also, for the earliest stages, Clark and Harris (1985), Perlès (1987), and James (1989).

4. Writers who have alerted me to this problem include (apart from Weber 1978 [1922]) McNeill (1963), Lenski (1966), Harris (1977), and especially Elias (1994a; 1987a). More recently I have come across the monographs by Glassman (1986) and Gellner (1988) which also deal incisively with the rise to power of priests.

5. The threefold formulation is by Talcott Parsons. See Goudsblom (1980, 69).

6. "One should . . . not be surprised to find that these leisured priests-elders would increase their skills and knowledge in manipulating people and use it to elevate further their own position so that they would emerge as the first aristocracy, the first upper class, the first ruling stratum" (Glassman 1986, 2: 33).

7. Thus, to give just a few examples, Gerhard Lenski, one of the few sociologists who have addressed the problem of priestly rule as a general problem of social stratification, defines priests as "those who mediate in the relation between God, or the gods, and man in the performance of holy rites" (1966, 256). Likewise Norbert Elias, who cannot possibly be suspected of theological leanings and who has insisted even more strongly than Lenski that the problem is to be seen as one of social power, writes that "the power of priests was derived in the first place from their special relationship with the gods" (1987a, 241). In a similar vein Johnson and Earle write in their excellent monograph on the evolution of human societies: "Descended from gods and invested with special powers, the chief has the final say in all matters involving the group, including ceremonies, adjudications, war, and diplomacy" (1987, 318). From an archaeological atlas I quote: "The administrative demands of the growing population led to the rise of bureaucracies and encouraged the adoption of writing. Professional priestly classes came into being to regulate relations with the gods" (Scarre 1988, 103); "Each city (in Mesopotamia) was under the protection of a particular god, housed in the splendidly fitted main temple along with his numerous human retinue" (Scarre 1988, 124). Finally, to conclude this arbitrary collection: "Yet always beneath both Mexican patriotism and the rational goals of the state were the insatiable demands of the gods. The pantheon's need for an ever greater number of sacrificial offerings required unceasing warfare to obtain captives" (Conrad and Demarest 1984, 44).

8. See, for example, Boserup (1965); Sahlins (1972).

9. In the concepts "ecological regime" and "agrarian regime" as I use them here, the meaning of the word "regime" is not confined to the common dictionary definition of "mode of rule" or "prevailing governmental system." My use of the term "agrarian regime" is compatible with Marc Bloch's view that "Each [agrarian] regime is an intricate complex of techniques and social relations" (1966, 35). The term is intended to refer to a concept of the same order as the concept of "medical regime" as developed by de Swaan (1988) and "religious regime" as developed by Bax (1988), both of which are elaborations upon Elias's (1994) theory of the interplay of "internal" and "external" constraints.

—————— Chapter 3 ——————

The Formation of Military-Agrarian Regimes

Johan Goudsblom

Ever since the domestication of fire began, a steady undercurrent in the development and history of human society has been the extension of human hegemony over other species. With the emergence of agriculture and pastoralism, this trend entered a new stage, as some species (the domesticates) were now protected and brought under human control, while others (the remaining wild species) were—if not exterminated—more or less effectively kept away from the expanding human domain. Almost inevitably, the availability of more land that people could exploit exclusively for themselves and their domesticates resulted in population growth—a process to which some biologists might refer as increases in human biomass, and which Eric Jones and other economic historians would call *extensive* growth. In a few cases, moreover, an increasing supply of goods per capita, or *intensive* growth, was obtained in the long run. Almost everywhere in the development of agrarian societies, however, the gains that were made in material prosperity tended to be distributed very unequally over the population.

The Stratification of Agrarian Societies

Increased productivity at this stage did not engender a general rise in the standard of living but resulted rather in a process of increasing social stratification—of differentiation of people according to power, property, and prestige. As noted before, the four major categories that emerged were those of peasants; craftsmen and traders; priests; and warriors. All over the world and in different historical eras, a similar fourfold division of social categories arose, with similar hierarchical implications. Regardless of the enormous variety of its specific historical guises, this was the basic pattern of stratification in a wide range of agrarian societies, from ancient Mesopotamia to pre-Columbian Mexico and Peru, from preindustrial Britain to preindustrial Japan, among the Celts and among the Ashanti.

In all these societies the majority of the population consisted of peasants: they tilled the soil and were at the bottom of the social hierarchy. Craftsmen and traders were far fewer in number. Some of them might attain considerable wealth but they rarely rose to the highest ranks. The supreme positions in the hierarchy of power, property, and prestige were monopolized by priests and warriors. This is not to say that all priests and warriors were rich and powerful. Many of them were hardly better off than the poorest peasant. The point is that the ruling elites were composed of priests and warriors and—in some very advanced agrarian states—their descendants.

In the previous chapter, on ecological regimes and the rise of organized religion, I tried to explain how priests could become so powerful. Here I turn to the warriors. My explanation will run along parallel lines. It will focus, again, upon the emergence and subsequent development of agrarian regimes.

Agrarian Regimes

Productivity and vulnerability—this combination of conditions under which peasants had to live—forms, in my view, the key to understanding the common underlying power structure in advanced agrarian societies.

For societies which embarked on agrarianization there was, in the long run, no way back—if only because increased productivity tended to lead to an increase of population and a decrease of wild territory in which people could find their subsistence by gathering and hunting.

As a consequence, peoples engaged in agriculture increasingly found themselves compelled to live under a new form of ecological regime—an agrarian regime. They simply had no choice. In the previous chapter I have sketched what was probably the oldest form of such a regime: the religious-agrarian regime, led by priests. Wherever these *religious-agrarian regimes* were established, however, they found themselves in the course of time in competition with, and having to make room for, *military-agrarian regimes,* led by warriors. I use the term "make room for" because this leaves open a great many possibilities, ranging from the virtual elimination of an authoritative priestly class—as in ancient Greece and Rome—to all sorts of shared dominance, such as the co-existence of "secular" and "spiritual" elites in medieval Europe.

To be sure, the emergence of military-agrarian regimes was a dominant, not a universal, trend. There are indeed documents from societies with rather intensive agriculture in which hardly any mention is made of either priests or warriors. One such document is the didactic poem *Works and Days* by Hesiod, the Greek poet who lived around 700 B.C.[1] He begins by avowing his distaste for military strife. It is much better, he says, for people to compete in peaceful pursuits: let potters vie with potters, in skill, and bards with bards. Hesiod himself, as a bard, sings the praise of the old agrarian virtues of diligence, thrift, and social responsibility. He does so, however, without any reference to priestly guidance. Instead, he urges his listeners and readers to restrain their impulses toward idling, squandering, and quarreling *of their own accord*—because it is, after all, in their own interest. In other words, Hesiod commends an agrarian regime relying upon self-restraint, not unlike the moral regime of self-restraint that Max Weber (1904–5) described as "the Protestant ethic."

I shall return to Hesiod later. I have mentioned him here as representing an extreme case—a highly exceptional and intriguing deviation from the way agrarian regimes were maintained in most parts of the world most of the time.

Far more typical was the social world evoked by the other great early Greek poet, Homer. Consider the following passage from the *Odyssey:*

> The same wind as wafted me from Ilium brought me to Ismarus, the city of the Cicones. I sacked this place and destroyed the men who held it. Their wives and the rich plunder that we took from the town we divided so that no one, as far as I could help it, should go short of his proper share.[2]

Clearly, these are the words of a warrior. The narrator is Odysseus, and the casual, matter-of-fact way in which he tells us what took place when he happened to land at Ismarus gives us an impression of how he and his men used to go about during their overseas wanderings: pillaging and plundering. But then, just like the peasants tilling their soil, they seemed to have no other choice; this was their way of making a living.

The latter may be slightly exaggerated: the Cicones had been allies of Troy, and Odysseus might have felt justified in treating them as his enemies. At the opposite pole, he might find a hospitable welcome in the palace of a friendly lord. Such a generous reception would only be given, however, on a basis of reciprocity by men of equal rank—by noblemen, wealthy and reputable warriors capable of holding their own and, if challenged, defending their honor in combat (cf. Finley 1977).

It is interesting to compare the actions of Odysseus with those of the Krobo priest to whom I referred in the previous chapter, who would serenely climb up to his vantage point on the mountain every morning in order to watch whether the time for sowing had come. As they are portrayed in the stories that have come down to us, both Odysseus and this priest knew, each in his own way, how to command authority. They did so, however, in very different capacities: the one as the leader of military operations, the other as the leader of religious rituals. They represented almost as antipodes the two types of rule by warriors and by priests.

As I said before, we should not draw too idyllic a picture of the part played by the Krobo priest. According to the account of their chronicler, the Krobos originally came from Dahomey; they had fled because they found the rule of the king of Dahomey too oppressive. While on their way they engaged in battle with other peoples; after many wanderings and conflicts they finally found a home on the heights of the Krobo mountain (Azu 1929, 6–10; see also Huber 1963).

The entire history, told in a few pages, is remarkably similar to the adventures of the people of Israel as told in the first books of the Old Testament. No more than the ancient Israelites did the Krobos live in a society that was free from war. However, they had managed to find refuge in an area where war was not endemic, and where the priest could assume leadership in the rituals of agrarian life. They had found relative peace for a while, beyond the reach of the military-agrarian kingdoms of West Africa. But even here they had to contend with forces which were conducive to war. Thus, our chronicler tells us, in a neighboring tribe the chief was so belligerent that his own people, in order to stop him from drawing them all into war, chopped off his right hand (Azu 1929, 9).

Intermezzo: The Reception Effect and Its Implications

This anecdote raises the question of the degree to which war, or religion, is "natural" and "universal." I shall diverge from my actual subject for a moment to address this question, and discuss briefly the "reception effect." It is very simple; everyone who has ever attended a reception is familiar with it. When the first few persons enter the room where a reception is going to be held, they can carry on a conversation in a normal voice. As more people come in to join the party, however, the volume of noise in the room increases; and in order to make themselves understood, people have to continue raising their voices—thus adding more and more decibels to the general murmur. After a while everybody is speaking at the top of his voice, and nobody can really understand what the other person is saying.

Does this mean that human beings have a natural propensity for talking as loudly as they can? No. The moral of this digression is clear: it is the pressure of the social circumstances—or, to put it more learnedly, the dynamics of the social figuration they form together[3]—that makes people raise their voices. Everyone is shouting because everyone else is shouting.

A full recognition of the social mechanisms at work in the "reception effect" is conducive to the methodological stance of taking nothing in human conduct for granted as it is. The volume of noise produced in the reception room at any given moment can only be explained as a function of the process of "noisification"; after a while, it has passed its peak, and "denoisification" sets in. The same observation applies to a great many other social processes, including militarization and pacification. There is no reason to regard a continuous state of war as the "natural" condition for human beings to live in—nor is there any ground for making such a claim for the opposite: the ideal of paradisiac peace. The whole idea of a "natural state" in which human beings might ever have lived is highly dubious; for in which stage of social evolution should such a state be situated? It seems more reasonable to take a processual view and to suppose that there have been periods in human history when peoples in certain areas could live in comparative peace, and periods when they could hardly avoid becoming entangled in violent encounters. The explanation for the varying degrees to which groups felt—and actually were—threatened by each other cannot be found in an unchanging "human nature." Here again the adage applies that changes can best be explained by relating them to other changes.

There is another general principle that may be illustrated by the story about the unfortunate chief who could no longer pursue his war-like ambitions because his own people had mutilated him. What this tale points to is the presence, I daresay always and everywhere, of countervailing trends. And these trends should not be conceived of as abstract, almost metaphysical forces; they are embodied in concrete human beings—some of whom (as in this case) may be primarily interested in peace, others in war. The same tendencies may, of course, operate in the same persons, who will then be torn by conflicting motives. In any case, if in a society dominant trends can be observed tending in a certain direction, we are always well advised to look for countervailing trends as well, pulling people in other directions, and to inquire why the countervailing trends were outweighed by the trends that turned out to be dominant.

Stages in the Monopolization of Violence

Many societies have gone through periods—often prolonged periods—in their history during which wars were inevitable and seemed to belong to the natural order of things. This could be so even in the absence of a distinct class of warriors; in tribal societies, all the young men could be admitted to the warrior group after they had passed the proper rites of initiation. This was customary, for example, among most Indian tribes in North America, whom European missionaries described as being involved in annually recurring deadly struggles—struggles which would end in the most cruel humiliations and tortures of the vanquished.[4]

These tribal societies represented an early stage in a process that is still continuing: the monopolization of violence by organized specialists.[5] During the first stage of this process, which extends far back into hominid prehistory, group violence increasingly became a prerogative of men. Of course, women and children could never be completely kept from using physical force among each other and even against men, but they tended to be excluded from organized fights between groups. This process of division of social functions, with the concomitant differentiation of power, cannot be explained by physical gender properties alone. Thus, in many tribal societies it was strictly forbidden for women even to touch weapons or to take part in their manufacture (Harris 1993, 283). Such "taboos" do not correspond to any inborn abilities or disabilities: they reflect relations of social power which have evolved over time.

The second stage in the long-term process of the monopolization of physical violence was the formation of a class of professional warriors. The transition to this stage occurred in agrarian societies with an advanced specialization of functions.

There is some evidence to suggest that "priests" preceded "warriors" in forming a profession of their own. It would seem that in several parts of the world—in Mesopotamia, in China, and in Mesoamerica, for instance—the first cities were built around temples containing stores of food and other treasures. In view of the storage function of these temples I think it unlikely that they were ever entirely unguarded. The archaeological record appears to suggest, however, that initially they were not strongly fortified.[6]

What the record also shows, and more clearly, is traces of destruction. The first temples were burnt down, and when they were rebuilt, they tended to be walled. The temples evolved into citadels.

Then, at a later stage again, we may observe a demilitarization of the temples. In some cases this may reflect a genuine demilitarization of the society of which they formed a part. Far more often, however, the demilitarization of the temples (or churches) reflected an increasing differentiation of social functions, and a transfer of military power from priests to warriors. Temples became relatively peaceful enclaves in agrarian empires that did not lose their strongly military imprint.

Thus, as early as in the legendary era of Abraham, Palestine was a region that lay within the sphere of influence of military-agrarian empires; the vicissitudes of the people of Israel as described in the books of the Old Testament consist to a large extent of military events—battles, victories, defeats. The Babylonian captivity signified the definitive end of the sovereign military power of an Israelite state, and this military defeat gave new chances of power to the nation's spiritual leaders, the priests.

Greece lay more in the periphery of the great empires of Western Asia, but there, too, war appears to have been endemic most of the time. A farming life not menaced by war, such as we find depicted by Hesiod, was, in all likelihood, rare. As a true-minded farmer, Hesiod was given to bitter complaints about his terrible plight, but this should not blind us to the fact that his poem bears all the marks of having been written in what must have been an oasis of peace. It is altogether a fascinating source of sociological interpretation, and its author deserves to be regarded as the first ideologue of the Third Estate. Our main theme here is, however, the sociogenesis of the Second Estate, the warrior aristocracy.

Whereas Hesiod hardly refers to military violence at all, it is present in almost every page of Homer's *Iliad* and *Odyssey*. The subject matter of these great poems *is* war. The last sentence of the Book of Judges reads: "In those days there was no king in Israel; everyone did what was good in his own eyes." This sentence applies equally well to the world of Odysseus and his peers: they were unruly warlords who would sometimes join forces against a common enemy but who would in the last resort always be prepared to take the law into their own hands.

Is Homer then describing the "war of all against all"? Certainly not in any strict sense. For one thing, in the world of Odysseus, military force was already monopolized to a high degree—even if the monopoly was still very far from being as strongly centralized as it was to become many centuries later when the Macedonian kings Philip and Alexander established their hegemony over this area. At Odysseus's time, there was a small upper stratum of highly independent warriors who possessed the material equipment and—no less important—the physical and social-psychological skills, acquired through long and arduous training, which, in combination, were needed to fight a war. The large majority of the population did not take part in the struggles, and could only hope that they would be spared the fate of being raided by an armed band.

Increased productivity, greater numbers, and a higher degree of concentration, specialization, and organization all combined to enable people to exploit unprecedented technical possibilities. It was especially the forging of metals, made feasible by enhanced control over fire, which played a crucial role. Having been used at first mostly as ornaments and means of exchange, metals became increasingly important in the manufacture of tools for agriculture and even more so of weapons for warfare (cf. Tylecote 1987).

The emergence of a warrior class was not simply the function of technological advances in metallurgy, however. The new techniques in armor and weaponry as such were, in turn, conditioned by the increasing specialization of warriors. In tribal societies the warriors used to be part-time specialists. When there was farming work to do, they would do that (or, if they felt it to be beneath their dignity, they might go hunting). Usually, it was only after the harvest had been reaped that the men went to war. As men, they monopolized warfare, but war continued to be by and large a seasonal activity.

The shift that occurred in more advanced agrarian societies was the rise of full-time warriors—men whose prime occupation in life was not, as in farming, production, but its very opposite, destruction, and who were available for this purpose all year round. Warriors, military men, became professional experts in killing people and burning property, in murder and arson.

Although this may sound like a moral indictment, I do not intend it that way. I merely wish to make a very general factual statement. What specialized full-time warriors in advanced agrarian societies were good at, where their expertise lay, what their particular training, organization, and equipment enabled them to do better than nonspecialists was precisely this: large-scale murder and arson. By virtue of their capacity to kill and burn they could overwhelm an agrarian community, capture its property, and—literally—get away with it, the way Odysseus did after his seizure of Ismarus.

The three components—training, organization, and equipment—were, I think, equally important for the emergence of a warrior class. The training consisted not only in learning to handle the equipment of sword and shield, but also in acquiring the habits of command and obedience that were required of the military leader and his troops. Authority in command was necessary to plan the logistics and to coordinate the actual operations of combat as well as to prevent the soldiers from looting for themselves and, in doing so, turning against each other. Odysseus's assurance that after the sack of Ismarus no man went away without his proper share of the booty throws some light on this aspect of military discipline and the way it was sustained by hierarchy.

By themselves, the properties of the warriors as such cannot sufficiently explain their rise as a dominant social class. Several authors, such as the German historian Alexander Rüstow (1950) and the Dutch sociologist Anton Wichers (1965), have pointed out that the process of *Überlagerung,* as Rüstow calls it—the "overcasting" of agrarian society by an upper layer of warriors—can only be explained by the particular *bonding* of warriors and peasants, as protectors and producers. It was in this bonding process that military-agrarian societies took shape.

Although Rüstow himself does not use the concept of "military-agrarian society," he has clearly perceived the power relations underlying this type of society. For an eloquent sketch of the inextricability of these power relations, read the following quotation from Wichers:

The majority of the population had to live scattered and in small units, which considerably impeded popular communication and organization. Then there was the fact that the harvest and the livestock were so difficult to hide. That harvest, moreover, had previously stood in the field for half a year or longer, vulnerable to destruction. The rural areas lay as it were invitingly open for "lawful" and unlawful forms of coercion and tribute. Whoever had assembled some cavalry around himself and trained himself to use a sword could subjugate the sedentary population, either gradually from within or suddenly from without. The people, moreover, could not imitate this by equipping and training themselves, for then they would have to neglect their fields. We saw that there were few possibilities for a subsistence outside agriculture, so that the "saturation limit" of non-agrarians was soon reached. Consequently, there was also only limited room for lords or for cities with lordly ambitions. Once one had such a lordly position, one had one's competitors to fear, but no longer very much the great multitude of the people. The latter would usually rather surrender something than suffer anyone's "punishments." Up to the eve of the present century we may observe, therefore, that the frontiers of principalities and other units of rule could change without this making much of an impression upon the majority of the people, let alone their having been consulted. For them all too often it was merely a matter of being bitten by the dog or the cat. (Wichers 1965, 53)

In making these observations the author is primarily referring to rural Western Europe (and the Northern Netherlands in particular) in the Middle Ages and early modern times. If we replace the cavalry by differently equipped troops, however, his words can serve as a general characteristic of the power structure in the world of Odysseus and in a great many other settings.

The crucial point, for which history provides us with abundant examples, is this: an agrarian community was virtually defenseless against organized military bands—unless it could mobilize an army of its own. This observation, in all its simplicity, can serve to explain what seems to be the functional paradox of warriorhood: *the function of warriors was to fight against other warriors.*[7] The paradox is resolved when we relate it to the basic features of agrarian society. Farmers and peasants lived a life that was (comparatively) productive and vulnerable. Warriors, on the other hand, were unproductive and destructive but ready to fight. Innocuous as it is, this formulation conveys something that is essential to the structure of military-agrarian societies. Given the peasants' productivity and vulnerability and the warriors' powers of destruction and readiness to fight, a combination of the elements of productivity and armed force turned out to be well nigh inevitable for both groups. The warriors needed the peasants for food, the peasants needed the warriors for protection. This un-planned—and, in a profound sense, fatal—combination formed the context for the great variety of mixtures of military protection and economic exploitation that mark the history of the great majority of advanced agrarian societies.

At one extreme was the Odysseus-at-Ismarus variant: a single brief and violent visit to a community that did not enjoy sufficient protec-tion. The opposite pole was formed by the situation that is more famil-iar to us—of farmers who regularly pay taxes, who may have done some military service when they were young men, and who remain free from visitations by armed troops for the rest of their lives. In between these two poles we may find the finest gradations of looting, extortion, serfdom, and land rent, which form so many variations upon the common theme of the symbiosis of agrarian producers and their military protectors—as analyzed comprehensively by writers of such different persuasions as Eric Jones (1987, 1988), John Hall (1985), Michael Mann (1986), and Ernest Gellner (1988).[8]

Perhaps it might have been comforting if, at this point, I could say that in actual practice life was not as bad as all that for the peasants, because, after all, they still had their priests. If the warriors threatened to go too far in oppressing and pillaging, the priests would intervene and would, so to speak, chop off the right hand of the warriors.

This did not, however, happen very frequently. More often than not, priests and warriors would lend each other a helping hand. As far as I can see, wherever in agrarian societies rural settlements developed into city-states which were subsequently engulfed by larger empires, the priests became subservient to the warriors. This shift in the balance of power occurred equally in those cases where the ruling ideology (which usually was a religious ideology) might give a different impres-sion, suggesting that it was the priests who formed the First Estate or the highest caste.

I do not think that the great antipriest, Friedrich Nietzsche, was correct when he proposed that at first there was a regime of warriors that was then taken over by priests through cunning and deceit.[9] If there was a clear succession, it is much more likely to have been the other way around: as societies increasingly came to rely upon crops and livestock, religious-agrarian regimes emerged which later were superseded by military-agrarian regimes. The military elites, understandably, did not always manage to establish working relationships of mutual trust with the majority of the population. This may help to explain their willingness to enter into coalitions with priestly groups who, in their disciplinary role, stood closer to the people and had a firmer grip on them.

Further Developments in the Relations Between Priests and Warriors

This, then, is how we may envisage the sociogenesis of the three orders. It all began with the intensification of agriculture, which offered special power chances to priests as specialists in orientation and discipline. They helped to subordinate individual to collective interests, and short-term to longer-term interests; this important social function formed the basis of the religious-agrarian regimes which they conducted. However, as the productivity of agrarian communities increased—partly by virtue of the new ecological regime—so did their vulnerability to attack by armed bands. Moreover, in the process of specialization, new craftsmen emerged, such as smiths, whose mastery over fire enabled them to make weapons of a force and flexibility that enormously increased the destructive powers of the warriors. As a result, "militarization took command," leaving no single people unaffected. If a group did not wish to be captured by foreign invaders, it had to recruit military specialists out of its own midst who then were in a position to join the ranks of the warrior elite.

Along with the ascendancy of warrior groups the religious-agrarian regimes were weakened in another way as well. Agrarian life had long ceased to be a novelty; the need for priestly guidance in sowing and harvesting and in slaughtering animals diminished. Like Hesiod, farmers could handle these tasks themselves.

We can see how, as a result, the element of agrarian discipline gradually receded into the background in the repertory of priestly activities. Thus at the dawn of Christianity, concern with agricultural procedures had virtually disappeared. Christ himself is often said to refer to peasant life, but only for the sake of parables: just as the peasant will separate the wheat from the chaff, so, when the day has come, God will judge men, etc. Rural life had become the familiar context from which similes were chosen, but the problems of farming were not anymore the focus upon which the teachings concentrated.

At the time when Christianity originated, the agrarian regime was so firmly established in a combination of militarily backed external supervision and internal self-restraint that regular priestly support was redundant. Moreover, as concentration of the population proceeded, increasing numbers of people came to live in cities. Under these circumstances, the problems ensuing from the conditions of life in a large military empire took precedence over those of agrarian production and storage. It was primarily to the former type of problems that the teachings of Christ were addressed. Christianity and the other great world religions, as Max Weber argued (1978, 1: 526–76), are attuned to the ideal of individual salvation—an ideal that seemed particularly appealing to people who found themselves living under the continuous constraints of a society marked by enormous power differences and, concomitantly, very harsh social relations (as expressed, for example, in the gladiatorial games and in the public executions of prisoners— festive occasions which bear some resemblance to the human sacrifices of the Aztecs[10]). The central redemptory idea of a Kingdom of God—as a Kingdom—may be seen as an idealized reflection of the hierarchical structure of military-agrarian empires.

It remains intriguing that in the societies of the Greeks and Romans, in which for centuries the priestly class had been of little significance, a new priestly organization, the Christian church, succeeded within a span of less than ten generations in attaining influence over the highest state organs and in making its religion the official imperial cult. Even more intriguing is the fact that, when a large part of the empire collapsed, this priestly organization managed to come to terms with the new, "barbaric," military rulers.

Notes

1. On Hesiod, see West (1978). A highly readable translation of *Works and Days* is that by Dorothea Wender (Harmondsworth: Penguin Books, 1973).

2. Homer, *Odyssey,* prose translation by E.V. Rieu (Harmondsworth: Penguin Books, 1946), 9: 39–43.

3. Cf. Elias (1994, 213–15); Goudsblom (1977, 126–31).

4. See also Clastres (1980, 171–248). As Wolf (1982) and others point out, both the wars themselves and the way in which they were fought are to be seen in relation

to the pressures exerted by European colonists. Their influence on the American Indians may be compared to the impact of the Romans on the Germanic tribes in Northern Europe in the first centuries of the Christian era. The rise of religious leaders in times of military adversity such as the North American Indians went through is discussed by Wilson (1975).

5. On monopolization of military force, see Elias (1994, 335–439). It is important to note that the monopolization of military force, first by men, and then by a class of professional warriors, necessarily preceded the centralization of the monopoly in the process of state formation as described by Elias.

6. The indications for Mesopotamia include Wenke (1984, 249–67); those for China, Wenke (1984, 325–27) and Stover and Stover (1976, 25, 38); those for Mesoamerica, Conrad and Demarest (1984, 19 and [with some reservations] 88). While evidence for the historic priority of a "theocracy" (as rule by priests is conventionally but somewhat misleadingly called) appears to be less strong than earlier writers such as Adams (1966) and Wolf (1959) have concluded, the case for such priority has still been stated persuasively by Glassman (1986, 2: 25–34).

7. The nonteleological way in which the concept of "functions" is used here is further discussed in Goudsblom (1977, 175–80).

8. Armed struggles between peasants and warrior groups possessing a monopoly of superior military force have continued from the days of the Assyrians well into the twentieth century. A typical testimony of the power balances in such confrontations may be found in Winston Churchill's memoirs of his years as a military officer in India. His account of an expedition against the Pathans reads like an echo of the memoirs of Julius Caesar and other great military commanders:

> Sir Bindon sent orders that we were to stay in the Mamud valley and lay it waste with fire and sword in vengeance. This accordingly we did, with great precautions. We proceeded systematically, village by village, and we destroyed the houses, filled up the wells, blew down the towers, cut down the great shady trees, burned the crops and broke the reservoirs in punitive devastation. (1930, 162)

Accounts such as this provide the background for Churchill's observation that the British government in India was "patient because among other things it knows that if the worst comes to the worst, it can shoot anybody down." Churchill's statesmanship is expressed in the words: "So societies in quiet years should be constructed; overwhelming force on the side of the rulers, innumerable objections to the use of any part of it" (1930, 148).

9. Friedrich Nietzsche, "On the Genealogy of Morals" (1887), in Kaufmann (1968, 439–602).

10. Weber (1978, 1: 526–76). On the harshness of social relations in Rome, see Hopkins (1980) and MacMullen (1974). On the Aztecs, see Conrad and Demarest (1984).

————— Chapter 4 —————

Extensive Growth in the Premodern World

Eric Jones

This chapter is concerned with the underlying long-term trend of the world economy rather than the usual stuff of economic history, its recent fluctuations. The conventional wisdom is that the entire world economy was stagnant in all material respects until the Industrial Revolution. Although it is admitted that there were changes, these are taken to have been cycles of little lasting economic significance—they are seen as the counterparts of the inconclusive wheeling in Milton's battles of the kites and crows. However, following Goudsblom's precept that nothing is ever self-evident (see page 31 above) would lead us to question the interpretation of preindustrial economic activity as directionless.

Alongside the standard, ultimately stagnationist, view it is widely, and somewhat inconsistently, realized that in the long run technical, scientific, and even cultural lore did accumulate. This is shrugged off on the grounds that gross distributional inequities denied the average person a benefit. Such a view is beside the immediate point, which is that major implications would follow from demonstrating that total output and income grew, never mind what happened to the average.

What is urged here is that overall output has been rising for several millennia at least.[1] The world was not connected in a single economic system until quite recently but it is still interesting that we can detect a net historical tendency in its economic aggregates. It indicates that output in zones of expansion was steadily outperforming output in zones of stasis and contraction. We are on reasonably safe ground in asserting a growth in the total with respect to the last three thousand years, perhaps longer, although this is a period which has seldom been treated as a whole. Over that span of time the interest of the archaeologist or prehistorian more or less fades before that of the historian picks up. During the period the predominant form of economic growth was *extensive* growth, meaning that total rather than per capita output and income went up. Interesting questions follow: what produced the tendency; what impeded a flow-on to *intensive* growth (rising annual real output and income per capita); and what were the implications for the eventual achievement of *intensive* growth, since the background was expansionary, not stagnant after all.

Any account of economic history which is concerned with abstractions of this order over the whole world during several thousand years is bound to be schematic. If the account claims, as this does, that there was continual net change at the global level, it must seem to speed up glacially slow reality and overrun the known instances of economic retreat so as to appear like a jerky silent film. The analogy is close in that individual actors do not get a chance to speak. Nevertheless, there are advantages which would be eroded by elaborating the account to discuss the fate of individual states or social movements in the usual fashion of histories. The advantages boil down mainly to those of a bird's-eye view in which broad patterns and long trends are visible whereas in the customary close-up they may be dilated out of sight. Notwithstanding this, there is meant to be room in the scheme to fit in the preponderant facts, the examples of the central tendencies of the economic past.

Veils Round the Premodern World

A demarcation line or sometimes a hiatus between the interests of prehistorians and economic historians is not the only reason why the last three thousand years or similar tracts are seldom treated as single blocks of time, with effects fatal to the recognition of *extensive* growth. From our position in time, the entire history of the premodern world is obscured by a number of veils.

For a start, we live after the spread of industrialization. Even what we think of as remnant agricultural societies, which hint at what the peasant past may have been like, are touched by it. Indeed, they are clenched in the fist of the world industrial market economy. We have a better general model òf market economies than nonmarket ones because we do not have a good general appreciation of the state as an economic system. Indeed, as Perry Anderson (1974a, 404) has pointed out, precapitalist economies were less alike than capitalist ones: there has been a capitalist convergence.

We live, too, after the demographic transition which has lifted humanity out of the high birth rate/high death rate pressure cooker—or, as some think, made the cooker blow up.

Further, we postdate the era of Western imperialism, the "1497–1947" era which refashioned the extra-European world. Europe's empires, held in a cat's cradle of sea-lanes, distract attention from the history of the land empires which formed world affairs far longer.

All these things make our perception of the premodern world misty. Our view of it also recedes very rapidly. According to a study by Taagepera and Colby (1979, 907–12) of the history of encyclopedias, which they take as summing up the perceived relative significance of knowledge, historical writing suffers from a steep and uniform rate of discount. As we go back in time, successively earlier periods receive less space. This is apparently on the assumption that the relevance or present value of the past is perfectly correlated with its nearness to us. It is a somewhat arbitrary assumption. Early periods of great technical change or institution building, perhaps the establishment of whole new cultures, may have been more formative than humdrum later times.

Demographic history definitely shares this recency bias, together with a yen for an exactitude seldom obtainable even in the developed countries before the census in the nineteenth century. According to one of them, Durand (1977, 253), demographers have a myopic view of history stemming from an excessive concern with measurements more precise than our macroeconomic models can cope with or strictly need. According to two others, McEvedy and Jones (1978, 358), historical demographers like best writing papers—"long papers, on small subjects, with no conclusions. Hunting about for the few that are relevant to a simple study like ours is an exhausting business." What is more, the short-period bias in demography seems to have bred an excessive interest in the social controls keeping fertility and mortality in balance, i.e., a positively economicslike concern with equilibria. In the *very* long term the world demographic condition has been one of *disequilibrium,* or the total population would not have kept growing. The equilibria to which premodern populations supposedly insisted on returning lay on an ever-rising curve.

The list of motes in our eyes is quite long. Our view of world history, or human history, suffers from the *parcellement* of nationalism. This is largely the result of Western historiography, self-absorbed, prone to treat that peculiarly Western creation the nation-state as the natural unit of human affairs. This political box has been exported so as to form a grid over the whole surface of the earth. Non-Western parochialisms and insularities have not shrunk from adopting the format for writing their own histories.

Yet, even in Europe, the nation-state does not have a particularly long history. The history of whoever happened to live in an area currently bounded by the frontiers of a nation-state is not at all the same thing. Writing that is to commit an anachronism, to fake the ancestry of the nation and the state as some people have been known to fake their family trees. The most serious consequence is to shatter the mirror that was formerly held up to global, or human, history. Seventeenth- and eighteenth-century scholars were properly interested in the whole world, or all humanity, as well as its parts. The looking glass they used needs to be glued together again if we are to detect the broad trends. Fortunately, the revival of "world history" to which this volume is a contribution suggests that this is happening.

All these impediments to a clear, farseeing, and complete view of the human past are influenced by the values of the observer. I do not imply willful kinds of blinkering, much less that there is one dominating ideology. Studies of single aspects of the past, from a particular direction, are appropriate in their place. Nevertheless, taken together they do blur whole world trends like the trend of *extensive* growth. Even to seek for something like this has been suspected as condoning growth for its own sake. There is a non sequitur here. It is by no means necessary to approve of something in order to think it important enough to study: who except neo-Nazis or Marxists could otherwise write the histories of Auschwitz or the Gulag Archipelago? Like mass incarcerations, growth is something the historian can observe. I happen to view one with horror and the other with qualified approbation, but the questions about both are the standard trinity of (social) scientific ones: What caused them? What did they involve? What were their effects? The answers ought to be as dispassionate as we can make them. We can and should allow explicitly for the influence of our own beliefs, as part of the long-standing search for interpersonal knowledge.

It is surprising to find that, after all the arguments, certain scholars persist in not agreeing that economic growth (meaning primarily the *intensive* growth which characterizes most of the world today) is a "good thing" and will be so for any foreseeable future.[2] After all, it is a maxim of welfare economics that more income is better than less. Achieving the "stationary" economy that is sometimes talked about—stationary, that is, in terms of average income per head—would be possible only if the number of downwardly mobile losers balanced the gainers. There is no chance that all incomes can be held rigidly constant, over the life cycle, for instance. Even trying to rig the books so as to maintain a net balance, with its gainer/loser implications, would be abhorrent to me, requiring as it would the imposition of force by the state. We have seen the deleterious effects of income rigidity on incentives in Brezhnev's USSR, and even there strict income equality was not the goal of the *nomenklatura*.

The arguments for growth have been stated by Sir Arthur Lewis (1955) and Wilfred Beckerman (1974). They seem clear in terms of minimizing the number of dead babies and giving everyone the widest possible choice, including the choice of leisure. The negative externalities of growth, which are more widely discussed than its benefits, are actually unintended outputs of given technological forms of production. They can and should be dealt with by changes in price incentives and the institutional structure. They are seldom as widespread as critics contend (this is another result of the common lack of a global perspective), nor (despite inevitable trade-offs) do they ipso facto negate the material and social value of growth.

The Case for *Extensive* Growth

The logic of the case that *extensive* growth has characterized the world economy for a very long time is that the rise of population must carry up with it total output, which implies total income. For this to be so, we need make only a minimal assumption regarding the initial annual average level of per capita real income, i.e., that it was very low, offering little room for any fall to offset a rise in the total produced by population growth. This assumption seems reasonable for the largely agricultural world of three thousand years ago. In my view it would also be reasonable for the world of hunter-gatherers but this is more contentious in view of romantic opinions about their lifestyle. Observations about that are not part of the case here, neither for the moment is any particular view taken as to whether it was population growth that pushed up total output or whether population was pulled up by output growth. Given that no decline in average real output per head would have been sufficient to cancel out the total effect of prolonged population growth, it follows that *extensive* growth did take place. The increase of population tracks a lower-bound for the growth of total output.

We possess estimates within appropriate bounds of plausibility which show that world population climbed 1700 percent from 50 million in 1000 B.C. to 900 million in A.D. 1800 (McEvedy and Jones 1978, 343–44). That is an annual growth rate of 0.103 percent. The most comprehensive and convenient source, the work of McEvedy and Jones, gives estimates which show that aggregate world population has grown for at least seven or eight thousand years. Since A.D. 500, at any rate, the aggregate growth has not paused for as much as a century. McEvedy and Jones claim that the indifference range, where there is no reason to prefer one figure over another, was no greater than 10 percent as far back as A.D. 1. They further calculate that the rate of growth reached its prehistoric peak about 1000 B.C., at the start of the Iron Age in Europe and the Near East, approximately the date when we will start our own survey. Although the rate slackened for a time, thereafter it remained positive and absolute numbers continued to climb as they had been doing and have done ever since.

It seems to be because rates of growth were low by the standards of very recent and atypical centuries and because there were marked variations in individual regions of the globe that the significance of the prolonged positive trend has been skated over. The doubling time has certainly been dropping. The total took from the start of the Christian era to the early fifteenth century to achieve one doubling; the next took only until 1750; the next again until 1890. This concentrates interest on the acceleration in the industrial era but it should be of deep interest that there was trend acceleration long before that.

Population growth without any sign of a long-term fall in life expectancy satisfies Guha's (1981) criteria for economic growth. These take human numbers and length of life as less chimerical indicators than utility maximization, where the goal indicator for currently preferred goods shifts up in Stakhanovite fashion with every advance. The criteria are (a) rising life expectancy with population constant, or (b) rising population with life expectancy constant, or (c) both climbing together. There are no satisfactory early data on life expectancy, but for what they are worth, the fragmentary samples collected by Dublin, Lotka, and Spiegelman (1936) from Bronze Age and Iron Age Greece, Rome, medieval England, and New England about A.D. 1800 imply an increase in life expectancy at birth from interval to interval over the whole period.

Coupled with the *extensive* growth inherent in overall population growth starting from a low income base, this implies that the world economy has been expanding for a very long time. There were more people for a start, while even if average real income per capita did not rise on an annual basis, the average person may have come to live longer. This does not mean that there was *intensive* growth in quite the modern sense, but it does suggest something subtly more than the minimum *extensive* growth criterion of greater total income. Perhaps we could call the *very* long-term average condition one of "*extensive* growth plus." This is consistent with the evidence of capital formation and economic activity in general. An eventual sea-change is indicated, overlooked though it has been.

Larger numbers and densities of people, with a slow swelling of output, necessarily expanded other variables. The context of all subsequent growth was increasing net investment and continual experience with technical change. The area cultivated had to rise at least in proportion to population, unless agricultural methods improved, which would be of interest in itself. The reality was a little of each: the areas occupied and cultivated rose and in major regions of the world agricultural tools, crop strains and species, and farming methods did all improve.

Agricultural intensification occurred in response to population growth even without the improvements in technique which we will in any case shortly describe. As Ester Boserup (1965) proposed, in agricultural systems with relatively little market activity, the cycle of shifting agriculture became shorter, and ultimately it was fixed to the spot. Whatever the trend of marginal returns to effort, i.e., output per person as opposed to output per hectare, there was the floor of subsistence needs underneath. This means that total output could go on swelling commensurately with the swelling of human numbers.

Capital in premodern times resided largely in cleared and fenced fields; herds and flocks of farm animals; and buildings of all kinds. We have nothing that passes for global estimates of these. Nevertheless, it is not only the logic of the thing which guarantees that they did increase. We have an extensive literature on the spread and greater densities of human populations; on conquests, frontier movements, and settlement histories; on vast irrigation works; and a considerable archaeology of buildings.

Despite this, the overall rate of capital formation was undoubtedly low. It is an easy sentence to write and easy to believe. But without the qualification, "by modern standards," it means little. Base-weighted in the long ago in order to observe what happened over time, rather than foreshortened by putting the base in the historically abnormal present, the salient fact is that the rate was positive rather than that it was low. For all the episodes of destruction, retreat, and genocide, there is no real doubt that the three thousand years before A.D. 1800 saw an enormous net accumulation of capital embodied in land improvements, in buildings, and in some other guises such as tools. Even very low rates, where they were invested in productive assets rather than in ceremonial structures, accumulated nicely over the length of time we have at our disposal.

Few people have ventured to cite numbers, though Goldsmith (1987) is a recent and valuable exception.[3] If we turn to the output side, to overall rates of growth in product per head, even Patel's (1964) figure of "less than" 0.1 percent per annum would mean that an annual share of total product of $50 per capita in 1000 B.C. would have become $821 per annum by A.D. 1800. The rate of 0.1 percent per annum derives from Keynes's essay on "Economic Possibilities for Our Grandchildren" (1951) and seems to be nothing more than an illustration or guess.

Goldsmith's figure of 0.2 percent per annum (1987, 233), which has the backing of the author's careful regional studies, would convert the same initial sum into $13,446 by A.D. 1800. That did not come about, of course. Goldsmith's phrasing at this point is untypically obscure. He may mean that the rate of growth of national product was no more than 0.2 percent per annum for periods of decades even when particular societies were doing well. It may have been lower, indeed it must have been lower, the remainder of the time, at least over the average of all societies. For instance, he thinks that the per capita share of national product in Mughal India in 1700 was about $200 (in 1970 dollars), about three-quarters of the then British, French, and Colonial American level. But the population of Mughal India was five times greater than the combined total of these other countries (Goldsmith 1987, 102; McEvedy and Jones 1978).

Keynes, who was so impressed by the power of compound interest, does not seem to have made much of the fact that the length of period he was discussing would offset, *ceteris paribus,* the lowness of its annual rate of growth. Nor did he make much of the need for a powerful explanation of why *any* positive rate did not result in a large final total. The time span is so great that minute variations in percentage growth rates, could they be sustained, would have made an enormous difference to the final figure. The rub is that they could not be sustained on the world scale, despite the evidence of innovative and expansionary activity.

Technical change in agriculture is undoubted. The stock of knowledge about productive techniques has been embodied in formal as well as informal sources for a long time back. The very term "Iron Age" marks a major diffusion of relevant lore. In Europe and China it came to be written in textbooks and *Nongshu* and updated from age to age. There were immense transfers of crop species and productive varieties. Consider three examples: the Arab agricultural revolution, which from the seventh century A.D. carried sixteen food crops from India as far west as Spain; the spread of Champa rice from Indo-China from the eleventh century and the successive rediffusions in China and Japan of strains that ripened earlier and earlier; and the "Columbian Exchange" through which not only were European crops and livestock established in the Americas but in return maize, peanuts, sweet potatoes, and white potatoes rapidly penetrated the agricultures of Europe, Africa, and China. The productivity effects of these technology transfers are well known. A wider range of cultivated species reduced the risks of harvest failure and acted as a demographic buffer. White potatoes, for example, were valuable in the hitherto climatically marginal northern tier of Europe while maize was useful in the dry Mediterranean basin.

Over the period there was similarly a disproportionate growth of cities. "Pre-modern history," declares Rozman (1973, 13), "can be seen as successive additions of new levels of cities." During the three thousand years to A.D. 1800 the share of the world's population living in cities of over 10,000 inhabitants went up from less than 1 percent to 4 or even 6 or 7 percent.[4] Ten thousand is, of course, a high threshold for premodern urbanism and probably does not faithfully indicate the scale of the withdrawal of labor from primary production. The increase has been dwarfed by the subsequent helter-skelter urbanization but, viewed fairly, it represented a considerable change in its own right.

This may have taken a long time, yet the urban proportion was much greater at the end than at the beginning: he who laughs last laughs longest.

Urbanization can be seen as part of a process of structural change, in which more and more labor shifted from less productive primary occupations like farming to more productive secondary (manufacturing) and tertiary (service) activities. This is consistent with an *absolute* rise in agricultural employment while nevertheless a smaller *fraction* of the population remained on the land to feed an increasing number and proportion of city dwellers. Better communications and marketing arrangements were also involved. While this structural shift has been eclipsed by nineteenth- and twentieth-century industrialization, once again it represented a profound economic change on its own terms.

There was yet another profound *very* long-term change, this time in the size of political units. Work by McEvedy and Jones (1978) and Taagepera (1978) shows that the largest empire in the world was always greater in both area and population than the previous holder of the title.[5] This conclusion is based on careful measurements of the geographical extent and estimates of population in successive empires. The empire was the typical large political unit of this phase of human history. In spite of the attention which, ever since Ibn Khaldun's day, the fall of empires has drawn to the dynastic cycle, the underlying trend of growth in unit size is conspicuous. In the literature there occurs the notion of an equilibrium size of political unit, a point at which costs and benefits balance, but like those of premodern populations, these equilibria lay on a rising scale.[6] The long-run condition of world society has been disequilibrium.

Despite a degree of obscurity surrounding the relationship between size of polity and *extensive* economic growth, a few suggestions may be made about possible connections. First, despite the slaughter associated with initial conquests, the internal order imposed by a single ruler quickly fostered population growth and economic activity. Second, some empires made strenuous efforts to promote economic stability by counterdisaster measures such as ever-normal granaries. The role of the premodern ruler typically included an insurance function of this kind; by the eighteenth century A.D., the measures in China in particular were most effective, having been developing on lines laid down under the Song eight or nine centuries earlier.[7] Third, international trade flourished best when it could take place between extensive, stable units, as in Han-Parthian-Roman or T'ang-Abassid times (Curtin 1984).

Most interesting of all, the "mean time to failure" of empires seems to have fallen in prehistoric times but become longer again during the Christian era. Between 2800 B.C. and 610 B.C., the first nine of a sample of eighteen empires shrank below 80 percent of their maximum extent after an average of 260 years, whereas for the last nine this took only 110 years.[8] Much later, the Asian empires supposedly damaged by Western imperialism were not only bigger than their predecessors but lasted longer. A way to rescue a hypothesis of Western malignity might be by arguing that those which survived did so because the Western powers propped them up. For the Ottoman empire, the "sick man of Europe" during the nineteenth century, this rings true enough, though by then the Ottomans were shedding territories and population. The same is not plausible with respect to Manchu China, the largest land empire of them all. Over the long haul of human history, empires—or top empires—had tended to expand in size and population.

In sum, what we observe in respect of *extensive* growth is first its sine qua non, the *very* long-term increase in population; second, ample evidence of agricultural expansion and intensification, together with the growth of cities, meaning all told a rise in world capital stock; and third an expansion in the area, population, and longevity of the largest political unit. The relationship between politics and economics cut both ways. Political expansion seems to have favored economic expansion even though it was also associated with the more familiar stagnation of per capita real income. These trends and relationships are detectable very far back in time, with noteworthy signs of accelerating gigantism in polities and economies during the eight hundred years or thereabouts before the classic Industrial Revolution of the eighteenth century A.D.

None of the fluctuations, regressions, or cycles of history were sufficient to halt or reverse the average trend of *extensive* growth. In a series of larger and larger regions of the earth, investment growth prevailed—on average. Likewise, states arose—and rose. Tainter (1988, 3) notes that the rise of the state has received far more attention than the fall. That is understandable. In the long haul, political expansion and recrudescence have dominated collapse. One hesitates to categorize major events such as the Fall of Rome as little local difficulties, but to do so might dramatize the point.[9] Furthermore, as Tainter observes, Dark Ages were seldom somber for everyone. Distant trade may have suffered from the collapse of imperial order; total farm output and on-the-spot consumption did not necessarily follow suit. What is odd is that this has not been thought of as an aspect of the underlying economic phenomenon: the ratchet effect of economic expansion has not received attention comparable to that lavished on the fortunes of the state.

Causes

The issue is, what was responsible for the *extensive* growth tendency? Given the central role we have assigned to population, it may be thought that an intrinsic biological urge in our species was responsible. The natural history or social biology of our species has certainly gained a vogue (Mackenzie 1978). One can identify any number of motives, along the lines of old age insurance, why the majority class of peasants may have chosen to form families and produce sizable broods of children. I have counted seven distinct reasons in the literature and some of these may have operated in combination. But such reasons tend to be social or economic as much as or more than biological; it is by no means clear that humanity inherently prefers to maximize numbers rather than income per head, or by virtue of biology alone is in a position to maximize either. It is not self-evident that we are or have been in the grip of some biological or demographic "manifest destiny" that must lead to numbers above replacement. Whatever the urge, social conditions affect whether it will be manifest.

It takes two to tango: both humanity and environment, the latter including competing peoples. Despite the adaptability of *Homo sapiens,* there seems no certainty that the environment or interspecific competition (i.e., other people) must sanction unending population growth. Admittedly, determinism of the control-by-sunspots kind is not quite dead. Climatic historians are most tempted by it, though nowadays they tend to dance away from the implications of their earlier statements.[10] Even Braudel's allusion to population fluctuations in China, India, and Europe being synchronized by unobserved fluctuations in the jet stream, "as if all humanity was in the grip of a primordial cosmic destiny in relation to which the rest of its history would be truly secondary" (quoted by Cameron 1970, 457), is protected by its rhetorical "as if" phrase.

There does seem to be one biological mechanism which permits human populations to jump upward at intervals. This is the crossing of thresholds when a population has "tamed" some disease organism, relegating it from a serious hazard to a nursery ill. A succession of these relegations can be documented (McNeill 1979). The exposure of populations to new diseases introduces some of the characteristic discontinuities of "real world" history, as when the Black Death spread with the trade under the Pax Mongolica: the demographic consequences were out of all proportion to the tiny commerce between Asia and Europe. Pandemics may thus account for some of the hesitations in premodern demographic growth. The process was nonlinear as well as not really predictable. The world has reached the stage of microbial unification only relatively recently (Ladurie 1973). Nevertheless, here is an apparently biological process which seemingly gives rise to the conditions for a series of demographic spurts. A snag for biological fundamentalism is, however, that it required changing *social* conditions, in this case trade links, to spread the disease organisms.

One way of approaching the issue of causation is to note that neither the trend of *extensive* growth as depicted by the course of population nor the trend in the size of the largest political unit was uniform through time. Both were subject to irregularities, including an occasional brief downturn but more conspicuously some plateau. Patently, the forces driving these trends ran out of steam after periods of some centuries but subsequently recouped—or others took over—and pushed upward again. Although this might be consistent, admittedly, with variation in biological or climatic influences, it opens the way for an alternative interpretation. Cycles are also consistent with the history of social innovation, and that is better documented than the cloudy assertions of climatic or *Ur*-biological causality.

Taagepera, for example, has suggested historical developments that may account for the observed renewals of the expansion path of empire. He associated a sudden increase in the area of the largest empire about 2800 B.C. with the emergence of cities; about 600 B.C. with the discovery of the means of delegating power; and about A.D. 1600 with a revolution in the speed of communication. At times the conquerors sopped up more advanced technical and administrative methods from those they had overrun and then generalized them over wider areas: examples cited by Clough are Greece and Rome, the Manchu in China, and the Aztecs who took from the Toltecs what they had taken in turn from the Maya (Clough 1961). Discontinuities like these hint that changes in social and economic organization are not simply reflexive responses to growing numbers but have to be socially constructed, may be diffused, and are subject to diminishing returns. In principle, once *extensive* growth is disaggregated, it is likely to prove amenable to economic analysis.

What seems most likely is that the major variations in population, size of political unit, and total output were at base the result of different combinations of innovations in methods of production, distribution, communications, and political management. In other words, what is being observed are economic and political innovations, none of infinitely lasting potency, all finally subject to diminishing marginal returns. When the gains to any given cluster of techniques began to fall off, there was a pause until some other novelty took up the slack.

The essence is that, taking the world economy as a whole, combined technical and structural changes kept output up with the growth of population. Measured over more than individual macroregions and short cycles of time, the world was not Malthusian. Great regional famines there were, but it has now been shown that their demographic impact was far less than historians have always thought; the imprint of the greatest recorded famine lasted only a tiny fraction of the length of our period and then only in a given region (Menken and Watkins 1985).

At the global level, improvements in agricultural method kept just a mite ahead of the growth of human numbers. Let us continue to call this *extensive* growth plus. The increasing returns needed to achieve *intensive* growth were harder to attain or sustain. They were not, however, quite so hard that the world could be transformed only once, by the European Industrial Revolution.[11] Taking into account the giant disequilibria caused by our species entering and re-entering more and more unoccupied niches, the *very* long-term average may have been constant returns.

Already at the start of our period, few areas of the world entirely lacked people. The expansionary process involved better equipped, better organized societies recolonizing less densely settled areas, while less disturbed populations gradually intensified their methods of production. This, then, was an economic and political rather than biological process, brought about by groups whose power and numbers had been augmented by successful technical or organizational change.

Certainly the process can be seen in its biological aspect as a modification of habitats. By and large each change made subsequent ones easier: even the aboriginal inhabitants of the neo-Europes studied by Crosby brought about so many changes in flora and fauna that the subsequent entry of European agricultural colonists was greatly facilitated (Crosby 1986). Earlier historiography missed the significance of this pre-European landscape modification, which we can now see as a slow enhancement of what the classical economists called "capital-in-land." For all the episodic upsets of history, the positive changes—the movements of peoples, greater average density of settlement, upgrading of methods, and conversion of more and more land to arability—resulted in an accumulation of capital; in short, in material progress.

Progress is a distinctly unfashionable term nowadays when general historians make everything of the initial costs to aborigines of white settlement and nothing of the later gains. However, the European expansion represented only another phase in the long saga of the intensification of economic activity, a *recolonization*. Because of its closeness to us in time and political importance, it tends to obscure prior movements, yet it was not new in principle. Stand back far enough, as we can from the end of three thousand years, and progress—material progress—is a reasonable description of the trend.

Structural change was more than a proportionate response to population growth. The rise of cities and increase in nonagricultural employment meant that labor was being released from farming. How was this done? Improvements in agricultural method must have been moderately labor-saving. Indeed, in most sectors, there were continual diffusions of technique, moving like glaciers but moving just the same. The westward spread of Chinese knowledge has been studied in greatest detail. As Glick (1979, 22, 132) has remarked, the Islamic Middle East, broker between Asia and Europe, rejected Chinese science but welcomed Chinese technologies, which could more easily be dissociated from any suspect ideological baggage. For many societies some fraction of technical change was thus exogenous. Boserup (1981) has also suggested that productivity gains were made endogenously because the big labor forces recruited to build irrigation works achieved economies of scale.

More fundamentally, technological change in general may have been weakly endogenous, an unintended by-product of everyday practice. Persson (1988) has formally urged as much for Europe. He believes that slowly accumulating technical knowledge was handed down from generation to generation in settled rural communities. The rate of change was governed by the extent of the division of labor, hence by the size of the market, and this in turn by the size of population. In this fashion the long-run growth of human numbers would automatically bring about technical change, sluggish but slowly speeding up, because it widened the market, increased the division of labor, and multiplied the chances of assimilating new skills by force of repetition.

There are difficulties with the Persson thesis. At the conceptual level, it is not clear why social institutions, including property rights, should not have played a major part in affecting the rate of technical change. On the empirical front, the larger populations do not necessarily seem to have been those with the fastest rates of change, and in addition there were undoubted regressions in technique at times. Nevertheless, in a general sense, the thesis sits well with the history of invention and innovation.

Elements of different explanations of *extensive* growth are lurking here. One is a demand-side explanation which simply assumes a tendency for population to grow and feed itself. In Boserupian fashion, agricultural intensification responds to the rise of population, and population grows subject only to intermittent shocks as isolated populations come into contact and suffer mortality from unfamiliar diseases. The shockwave of mortality caused by the initial European expansion to the neo-Europes of the Americas, the Pacific Islands, and Australasia is the best-known example.[12] In general, however, the process is self-fulfilling, almost automatic, driven by population growth.

This does not, however, readily account for structural change. The alternative explanation is a supply-side one: that the global cycles of population and total output mark the diffusion of successive levels of technique, each eventually succumbing to the onset of diminishing returns. Even McEvedy and Jones, who turn to climatic change to account for the downturn in their primary population cycle about A.D. 200, invoke European technology and imperialism to explain the cycle from the fifteenth century A.D.

A neat fit between particular complexes of farming method and world population cycles is admittedly hard to establish. For example, the food-producing effects of the Discoveries, that is, of the Columbian Exchange and the new lands available to cultivate, were so lagged that they cannot have been the cause of the gain in total human numbers during the fifteenth and sixteenth centuries. Their main effects awaited the development of oceanic transport in the nineteenth century. One possibility is that the population growth of the early modern period was merely a bounce back from the Black Death, supported by creeping, overlapping diffusions of better farming methods. Agricultural history has scarcely been written at the appropriate level, let alone assembled on a world scale, and there are many patterns we cannot yet detect. Of the population growth and *extensive* growth, there is no real doubt.

The cycles were like the risers and treads of a staircase. Perhaps demand- and supply-side motors took over from one another to produce this result. Wavelike diffusions of new technology may have pushed up output (and pulled up population) until diminishing returns set in. Thereafter population growth fed itself at more-or-less static levels, and continued to replicate existing technology, until another "wave of gadgets" swelled. The term "wave of gadgets" is by courtesy of T.S. Ashton's schoolboy; "wave" is a little dramatic and "gadgets" should be taken to include new institutional arrangements.

Impediments to *Intensive* Growth

Given a degree of technical advance and structural change, what impeded transitions to *intensive* growth? Not excessive population growth, since this was vastly slower than modern rates and would not have imposed unbearable dependency ratios. The basic impediments seem rather to have lain in the intensely hierarchical politics characteristic of premodern times. Goldsmith has made some calculations of the inequalities of wealth and income in seven premodern societies, of which three are probably representative of the larger empires before each began to decay (Goldsmith 1987, Table 12–1). His figures show that the top one-thousandth of all families in Augustan Rome in A.D. 14 received 4 percent of total income. In the Ottoman empire about A.D. 1550 the share was 15 percent. The top ten-thousandth of families received 1 percent of income in the Roman case and 5 percent in Mughal India about A.D. 1600. For comparison, the top ten-thousandth of families in both India and England in the late 1970s received only—if that is the word—0.1 percent of income. In the United States their share was 0.25 percent. Those figures are still ten and twenty-five times the equilibrium shares, but they contrast very favorably with one hundred times in Rome and five hundred times in Mughal India.

Not much of the disproportionate share of wealth and income in so few hands in the premodern world was reinvested productively. Instead it was spent on luxury, display, and the militarism needed to extract a surplus from one's own people, as well as to extract rents by conquering others. Although rational for ruling groups and conquerors, this was a slicing of existing pies: it did little to help bake them. That the rate of capital accumulation was so low by modern standards is partly explained by this: the heaping up of capital in the *very* long term which happened is explained by the length of time involved. Most people had very little left over from their ordinary needs to invest and little incentive to take risks; in these circumstances the noteworthy fact is that net investment did keep expanding, however slowly.

The great inequalities hint at their own explanation and at the explanation of how few were the instances of *intensive* growth. They point to the fierce social and political controls that locked premodern economies into rounds of mere *extensive* growth. Yet, as we have urged throughout, in itself that was an achievement. The premodern world was not one of utter economic stagnation but a prolonged unfolding which added up to *extensive* growth plus, though it seldom tipped over in any region into a growth of average per capita incomes. Seldom— but not just in the one Industrial Revolution. The economic context was slightly more propitious than that. Admittedly, the world economy as a whole seems not to have grown in the per capita income sense. On the other hand, population growth and technical change did impart a momentum of continual expansion.

Notes

1. A preliminary version of this argument appears in E.L. Jones (1982).

2. See the annual *World Development Reports* of the World Bank for statistics on growth performance.

3. For estimates of the rates of capital formation in certain premodern economies, see Goldsmith (1987, 36, 101, 132–33, 202–3).

4. Rozman (1973, 6); Chandler and Fox (1974). The comment by Jan de Vries (1984, 18) that the Chandler and Fox data are "all but unusable" is a little severe, given our very general purposes.

5. I am grateful to Professor Taagepera for copies of his working papers.

6. See especially the first chapter of Elvin 1973.

7. As demonstrated in a La Trobe University Ph.D. thesis by my student, Zhou Linong (1990); see also Zhou 1993.

8. Calculated from Taagepera 1978, Table 6.

9. The Roman empire is exquisitely placed in context, and to some extent cut down to its proper relative size, in Sitwell (1986).

10. They have not, however, responded persuasively to the challenge by J.L. Anderson (1981). See, for instance, Galloway (1986).

11. The difficulties of raising output were exaggerated in the development literature of the 1950s, '60s, and '70s, two characteristics of which were their short-period focus and, seen in historical perspective, wanting all change overnight.

12. See the treatment by Crosby 1986.

———— Chapter 5 ————

Recurrent Transitions to *Intensive* Growth

Eric Jones

The central task of economic history is to explain transitions from *extensive* growth to *intensive* growth. All else is commentary. The small number of spontaneous examples of *intensive* growth implies that transition was a surpassingly difficult matter. Yet all parts of the bridge were not equally hard to build. Although history is niggardly with clues as to which were the hardest parts, the prelude of *extensive* growth suggests that achieving a sustained rise in average per capita GNP ought not to have been preternaturally formidable. In the pre-modern world there was technical change and what might be called "investment creep." The need was not to crank up completely cold economies but to pass already warm ones, in which total output and income were expanding, through the phase transition to the point where average income per head was growing. The normal explanations, embodied in Industrial Revolution studies, are inclined to talk as though the achievement burst on an economically stagnant world. They tend to be couched in terms of novel push-forces. Here the aim will be to look for a different type of explanation.

The East Asian Growth Pole

First, however, we need to discard the assumption that the transition was so very difficult that it happened spontaneously on a unique occasion: in eighteenth-century Britain. To think so succeeds in confusing (among other things) growth with industrialization. There was in any case more than one focus of growth in the world, as there is today.

Alongside the Western world of Europe and its overseas annexes there is now an East Asian complex which is growing faster, possesses the larger financial market, and, perhaps least acknowledged, has a longer if somewhat more interrupted history. Treating East Asia as entirely derivative, as is usual, traps us inside the diffusionist interpretation that traces all growth back to the Industrial Revolution and impedes our understanding of the process of growth in the round.

The common approach to East Asian growth in general economic histories is to restrict it to Japan on the grounds that growth anywhere else in the region is extraordinarily recent. Furthermore, the Japanese experience tends to be assimilated to that of the West—to the point of labeling Japan "Western"—along one or other of the following lines: (1) The diligence and thrift enjoined by Japanese ideals are taken to be an ersatz version of the Protestant ethic. Enough said: that brings growth. (2) Japan, like Europe, happened to be feudal. Again, enough said: feudalism eventually self-transforms into bourgeois capitalism, assumed in turn to produce growth. (3) The Meiji Restoration of 1868 brought about a growth some suppose to have been lacking in Japan hitherto. The new regime adopted industrialism in order to join a West it could not otherwise keep at bay. (4) Japan really achieved growth only after her prostration in 1945—by emulating, and later outclassing, the industrial practices of her American occupiers.

These interpretations, some more than others, allude to real historical events and processes. The construction placed on each of them depends, however, on making Japanese economic history a variant or descendant of Western economic history, which is regarded as the *fons et origo* of all true growth. If one is thinking only with respect to industrialization, or with modern magnitudes and modern rates of change in mind, it is easy to slip into the same habit. The choices of 1868 or 1945 as turning points are attempts to define the Japanese adoption of Western industrialism. Either date begins a diffusionist tale. The explanations in terms of feudalism or religious behavior are more ingenious without, however, elaborating much on the economic effects. They offer Japan (and Japan alone among non-Western nations) access to growth on lines sanctioned by the study of Western history.

That Japanese talents were purely imitative was a prevalent opinion in the West in the 1930s, with allegations that Japan's industrial wares were routinely stamped "Made in Birmingham" or some such. Perhaps they were: access to the protected markets of Western colonial empires in Asia was limited. We shall argue instead that Japan's growth was distinct from Europe's and arose primarily because the political structure imposed by the Tokugawa evolved to permit it. It was really in the middle reaches, from the Meiji Restoration to the early Showa era, that Japan borrowed factory industrialism from the West. The earlier evolution was like that of the West, but quite independent; what Meiji did was to give a massive statist and westernizing boost to already active market forces. What late Showa did, after the Second World War, was to beat the masters at their own game.

The outcome is Japan's world prominence, so colossal that some might be led to switch allegiance and turn Japanese studies into a monotheism to replace that of the Industrial Revolution. Within the East Asian sphere, Japan's scale could easily distort the study of economic history, unless we think determinedly about causes and rates of change rather than magnitudes. Consider: Japan's share of world GNP is approaching America's; her share of world exports is almost there. Vast Japanese capital transfers are vital to the United States. Japan has the largest bank in the world, the largest financial institution, and the largest company. Japan's tiny land area is valued at approximately twice the value of the United States. And so on.[1]

Despite this, if we want to understand how growth starts rather than how it may attain hypertrophy, the appropriate sphere of inquiry is East Asia as a whole. In particular, notice should be taken of the dynamic phases of Chinese history. At first sight this seems a blind alley since again "everyone knows" that until the last couple of decades economic success in Asia was granted only to Japan. There are, however, at least three ways of revolving the lens to display a different picture. One, to which we shall briefly refer again, is to consider that the economic condition of Manchu China was not quite as unpromising as most accounts surmise. That means ceasing to dismiss early periods as irrelevant before we have looked to see whether or not they really are. Another is to adjust the reportedly low growth rates to take account of gains in life expectancy (Usher 1973). There is every reason to think that the result would be to show much greater percentage gains since, at the least, 1949 than are revealed by conventional income measures alone. The third approach we have already mooted: decoupling growth from industrialization in order to search for the inception of growth as such.

Comparing the histories of *intensive* growth in Europe and East Asia depends in the first instance on which European chronology is adopted. Contradictory opinions are expressed, or more often implicit assumptions are made, as to whether growth came early or came late, came fast or came slow. The opinion of the quantifiers has stretched the Industrial Revolution toward the present like a cartoon cat, implying that the growth rate of industrial production did not accelerate much until well into the nineteenth century. That school of thought tends to ignore early change, when there are few predigested statistical series. A less articulate view, still apparently held among economic historians, accepts that real wages per head had been growing for centuries, though very slowly and perhaps not continuously, nor outside Britain and the Low Countries. We will incline toward this gradualist view of the timing and to an even broader view of the parts of Europe that were involved.

If the East Asian record is set against this latitudinarian version of the European experience, it displays the following characteristics: an earlier start, at least as early as the Song dynasties (A.D. 960–1279); an admittedly less continuous record in the sense that the flame flickered and the torch came to be borne by Japan rather than China; a strong rediffusion within East Asia; and nowadays a distinctly faster rate of growth in areas bigger than the biggest European countries. In the literature on world development these characteristics are seldom connected in a coherent sequence. Yet *intensive* growth was Chinese before it was European, and today, although of course the income base is vastly lower, growth rates in some huge provinces of China are again faster than anywhere in Europe. The skeptical Western view is that this cannot last and will not spread; also that the earlier history cannot matter. It has been the bane of development economics to take the short view.

The present chapter urges caution about dismissing China's prospects and disputes the idea that history cannot tell us anything of interest. Consider the extent of economic activity and the remarkable stock of so-called preindustrial techniques in late Manchu China. The political system was decayed and average incomes were undoubtedly low but this does not necessarily denote a society which was backward in all other respects. Viewed more kindly than usual, it was one with a great deal of energy and creativity. It is possible to conceive that what was chiefly required was the breaking of a political logjam, not the construction of an economic system entirely from scratch. Compared with some parts of the less developed world, China remained heir to a heritage that had once been most influential and might perhaps be reactivated.

The world historian W.H. McNeill (1982, 24–25) has seen the early picture more clearly than almost anyone. He envisages the original European growth as an epiphenomenon of Song commercialism. This is the reverse of the West-East direction of economic diffusion in recent centuries. It points to a more appropriate history that embraces sequential hearths of change. This is welcome, since economic history should not take as its goal explaining how any given economy attained a particular equilibrium. The mutability of the past means that it would be inadequate simply to replace a saga which culminates in the British Industrial Revolution with another which culminates, say, in the present strength of Japan. To do so courts being left high and dry by the next tide of economic leadership.[2] The proper goal is the study of the *process* of change, not constructing a teleology that leads to the transient prominence of this economy or that.

After the Song, China as a whole reverted for centuries to merely expansionary growth (Jones 1990b; Jones, Frost, and White 1993). At least sinologists do not claim otherwise. The regions may have differed but virtually until Republican times there was no clearly documented return to *intensive* growth overall. However, in Japan *intensive* growth picked up. While it has to be taken into account that Japanese culture derived from China, the evolution of her economy was different. Japan's growth may be traced to a slow start during or even before the Tokugawa period. This had massive eventual implications, not only for Japan today but also for growth in the "Little Dragons" of South Korea and Taiwan. Their development is to an important extent a spin-off from the immensely rapid achievement of modern Japan whose colonies we have noted they once were. The important point is that they are heirs to almost as long a tradition as if they had been Western colonies.

By endeavoring to make room for a separate East Asian focus of growth, we duplicate the active economic history we need to know and teach. This makes for greater realism; what it does not do is solve the problem of origins, or more precisely of causes, since—as Marc Bloch objected—origins may muddle beginnings and causes. Two patches of growth instead of a single one have to appear on our map of the world. Does this mean that we should then think that these, and only these, cultures were preadapted for growth? To do so would be even more cumbersome and difficult to believe than continuing to write and teach as though only Europe were preordained to grow.

Any such notion that certain parts of the world were inherently favored would dissuade us from looking for evidence of other early stirrings of *intensive* growth. There were some instances, however faint. Exclusive concentration on the British or European case has always distracted attention from the possibility of comparable achievements elsewhere and restricted our chances of understanding the fundamental conditions under which *intensive* growth may appear. Including East Asia as well as Europe widens our scope but there is no advantage in entering two blind alleys instead of one.

Europeans and East Asians cannot be shown to have been the world's only creative peoples. That would permit modern results to obliterate past efforts. The very idea is redundant and may be offensive. It is distinctly likely, for instance, that *intensive* growth emerged in the coastal trading cities or states of southeast Asia during (what was in European terms) the Middle Ages (Reid 1988). That this episode went into reverse in early modern times is beside the point. For a spell another growth pole was sketched on the map. Comparative work taking into account this and any other tentative examples will be more revealing of the circumstances under which growth arises and can be suppressed than work limited to the history of the great survivors.

This said, three major cases do stand out. They are Song China (from the tenth to the thirteenth century A.D.), Tokugawa Japan (from 1600 to 1868), and early modern Europe (from, say, 1500 to 1800). In each instance the stirrings of still earlier periods ought to be included in a complete account of the inception of growth. We shall be conservative and ignore them here.

We have used the term "inception." It would be unfortunate if this reinforced the common assumption of abruptness, of growth "taking off." Another undesirable assumption would be that growth was rare. The relevant processes of technical and institutional change are regarded as having been super-difficult. This impression can be created by the apparent fixity of institutions when incentives were limited, as they were for long stretches of the past: take, for example, the survival of the guilds in China and the Middle East. Yet in Europe, once growth began, the guilds lost their teeth quickly enough and there is no reason to suppose that they constituted a more formidable barrier elsewhere (E.L. Jones, 1987, 1988).

Looking over too short a period can also create the impression that growth is immensely difficult. This was the sense conveyed by the literature of development economics for a generation after the Second World War: the apparent sluggishness of development, as seen in close-up, was a convenient stick with which to beat the former colonial powers. Growth may have been frustratingly slow by ideal standards but we can now see that it was historically rapid. It was achieved simultaneously almost everywhere in the world, quite without precedent.

Explanations of Growth

Models of growth usually assume the success of one or another novel push-force. The postwar experience of the Third World is, however, a graveyard of hopes that some particular propellant might be effective. Earlier British economic historiography is similarly a cemetery for an array of suggested push-forces or positive shocks, none of them fully capable of accounting for growth in its industrial guise, let alone as a general process.

The array of proposals in the literature on Britain was not accompanied by any test to determine how we might select among them. Some decades elapsed before it was realized that many of the changes approximately contemporaneous with the Industrial Revolution were no more than fellow passengers, correlates not causes. Thus the acts of founding of banks or systems of accounting, sometimes portrayed as crucial for growth, were in reality adaptations to it. Banks arose to service an already swelling volume of transactions. As the realization dawned that substituting one push-force for another in a historical merry-go-round lacked persuasiveness, so the subject lost its fascination as a research field. British economic history marked time with evasive statements about the multiplicity of the forces that led to industrialization.

Even the underlying hypothesis that growth originated in an industrial revolution—it is no more than a hypothesis—is unhelpful. What it conjures up is a miracle of the laser-beam sort, typically the result of technical change, the steam engine, the spinning jenny, or something of that kind. When change is admitted to have been more gradual, it is made dependent on some autonomous cultural change, of which the Protestant ethic is the major example. But a gradualist stance was never attractive to the economics profession, involved as it was with incautious policy advice, or to an instrumentalist attitude to knowledge about the past. Certainly economists embraced the notion of a take-off far more closely than did historians. A self-referring element entered the study of development. Bouncing across time like a Ping-Pong ball, the concept of an abrupt transformation in the past shaped expectations about unheralded development in the present, while the aspirations returned to elicit from history an ever more abrupt curtain-raiser.

No explanation by analogy with the Industrial Revolution, no merely Western explanation at all, can be general enough to account for the process of economic growth as a whole. It cannot comprehend China and Japan as well as Europe; its ground rules can only relegate them to the role of offshoots of European growth. In no way can it cope with the realization that what is to be explained is a number of separate cases, maybe responding to comparable stimuli but not necessarily to common stimuli.

A mental experiment is required. Rather than continue to ransack ever dustier corners of eighteenth-century Britain for a fresh propellant, let us consider a simpler postulate. Let us assume that a propensity for growth has been widely present in human society. This does not commit us to a "neoclassical" maximizing position. Not everyone need be engaged in maximizing on every margin at once. All that is needed is to accept that a desire to reduce material poverty is commonplace in our species—as well it might be—considering that poverty exacts such a penalty in terms of dead babies, or at any rate of babies without shoes. A certain inquisitiveness about how things work—things, that is, including markets—and a modicum of human creativity are ancillary postulates.

An objection against postulating universal, or rather semi-universal, behaviors like this has been raised by Anne Mayhew (1987). She terms them Elemental Human Strategies. She argues that they must empty the interest from the workings of the economy and distract attention from the institutions which are the proper object of study, the true stuff of history. Despite her institutionalist critique, for which economic historians ought to have some sympathy, other approaches have not produced a persuasive argument. In the circumstances, the assumption of a "growth propensity" seems worth a trial. Let us see how far it will take us.

Consider the prevalence of attempts to bring about technical change. There is some reason to think that they were the results of a deep inquisitiveness and dexterity that could be and often were stifled or deflected but which in themselves did not have to be created or induced. Technical advances have been described as the result of "more love than purpose" (Smith 1981, 330). That love, meaning aesthetics, was more widespread than rationality is surely not hard to believe. In any case Persson has noted a continual slow change in technique in the settled rural societies of European history and he offers a model of technical change as endogenous—weakly endogenous or the outcome would be more noticeable than it is, but endogenous nevertheless (Persson 1988).

The way that all this was worked out in historical cases was indistinct, and indirect evidence has to be used to assess it. We have neither macrostatistics, apart from those put together by Goldsmith (1987), nor the means—any more than do other economists—of observing motivations directly. The best we can do is to examine material on technological and structural change with our behavioral postulate in mind. Technical change in itself does not guarantee the presence of *intensive* growth, but although caveats will have to be entered, it does presuppose vitality. Structural change involves the withdrawal of labor from primary production into the more productive manufacturing and service occupations. If technical and structural change both persisted vigorously for a century or more, there is reason to suspect that *intensive* growth was taking place.

Admittedly, much early technical activity was not materially productive. There was more invention than innovation, and invention without insertion into the productive system is sterile. The slogan of Radio Rentals in Australia today illustrates the distinction: "Soon as they invent it, we rent it." The company, of course, means "produce," rather than the "invent" required to rhyme, but it makes the point: invention without production, distribution, and consumption—without innovation, without use—is null and void for our purposes. The economic historian, then, has to investigate not so much past scientific inquiry or technical tinkering as the productive employment of what was discovered. That demanded a wider investment response. The factors impeding investment in new methods and the circumstances under which they were eventually demolished become central, as they do to the study of growth as a whole.

Even when invention was followed by innovation, much of it remained unproductive in any relevant sense. Technical change was directed toward military equipment, defense works, religious structures, and buildings for display. Look at the Seven Wonders of the World: only the Pharos of Alexandria seems useful. In other words, much of the innovation that took place was induced innovation, responding to the demands of ruling elites and the state. The major exception seems to have been agriculture, where more productive change took place than has been noticed. Historians show slight interest in agriculture and admittedly the evidence is hard to handle. Although the biological changes required by farming will have cumulated in the inventory of crop and animal species entering the modern period, these things left few remains attributable to each successive era. Inferentially, nevertheless, there was a great deal of development in farming, and because that sector was dominant in early economies, the exception is important. It is not, however, quite weighty enough to disguise the fact that much premodern technical change was unproductive.

Full-blown growth remained rare. This is no reason to suppose that an impulse toward growth was not present: how else to explain the persistent economic expansion of the world? Rather, the forces acting against a translation of the impulse into per capita growth were strong. This applies to more than technical change. For instance, when the constraints on market activity were removed, markets could expand at a stunning rate. As Ernest Gellner says, many societies learn market behavior with alacrity, once circumstances permit this or encourage it: "Single-end rationality may not be quite such a difficult accomplishment" (1988, 175).

Once we countenance this heterodox view of the past, with mutable processes and subterranean forces for growth working away, the significant issues before us change. They become, first, what forces were suppressing the growth tendency, and, second, what removed the negative forces in those successful cases that we do observe. In turning in these directions we may seem to grant more credit to economic success in past societies than their ingenuity actually produced. Small, isolated tribal societies indeed do seem to have offered too little scope by way of individualism or market opportunity and too much scope for social control. They lacked competitive stimulus and were prone to perpetuate the mediocrity for which Hallpike (1986) has stigmatized them.

On the other hand, larger societies offered much more scope. Their markets were potentially vast and they have a recorded history of technical innovation and diffusion, slow only by very modern standards. Structural change can be detected on occasion. A spillover into raising incomes per head was within the bounds of possibility. This is demonstrated in a paper by S.R.H. Jones (1988) on the way King Alfred and his children ended the cramping of growth in ninth- and tenth-century Wessex. That author's inclination is to stress the positive forces, the royal creation of public goods, in particular orderly markets. My own view is that these goods, although important, were secondary. They were provided after the key circumstances had arisen and the key decision had been taken, to wit that the worst arbitrariness was over and would not be reintroduced lightly. What came first was the discovery by rulers that military competition could best be met from a strong market base. The economic activity of their subjects was to be fostered and gently milked, not crudely exploited. Although it was always the exception, other rulers throughout history occasionally made a similar discovery.

Was it this that was responsible for releasing *intensive* growth under premodern conditions? I think it was but there are other candidates than arbitrariness for suppressing the emergence of *intensive* growth. Besides politics designed to slice up the existing pies rather than help bake new and bigger ones, the literatures of economic history and economic development reveal a list of other features that we may suspect were responsible for suppressing *intensive* growth, such as natural resource inadequacies, hostile cultures, and inimical systems of values.

Resource difficulties we can deal with rather summarily. Resources are functions of technology. The classic illustration concerns oil and the American Indians who could use only dribbles for cosmetics and medicine. For them it was no resource at all, not in the sense that societies able to produce lamps and engines made it a resource. Resource endowments are admittedly not totally inert. They do affect the relative costs of operating economies under any given system of technology. But neither the animating spark, nor by the same token the wet blanket that could stifle it, is to be found here. In any case, the economist would insist that trade is a substitute for resources.[3] What is needed is an explanation of variations in the rate of technical change, not of differences in resource endowment.

Cultural explanations which refer to the special privilege or talent of particular peoples are also unsatisfactory. The frequent attempts at explanation of zero *intensive* growth in terms of supposed constants such as Confucianism cannot account, say, for both income growth in Song times and its apparent overall lack under the Ming. Neither does a common Confucian heritage sit well with the divergent economic performance of mainland and overseas Chinese during the first half of this century. At the very least something else must have mediated any Confucian effect. Shifts in the external context do seem to modify the practical content and operation of value systems in general. Alfred Marshall was especially perceptive about the way in which custom can be hollowed out by changing circumstances, its content remolded inside an antique dress. Ceaseless adjustments take place, even as to which precepts from the bodies of didactic or religious writings are selected to rationalize practice, though as Kuran (1988) has recently pointed out, most theories of cultural conservatism overlook the feedback from actual choices to preferences. The theory of cognitive dissonance is one attempt to explain how events may modify beliefs. No doubt reasonable people will find that reality involves an interaction. Yet that would be quite different from the vastly influential Weberian style of approach in which beliefs are autonomous and it is they which drive history by causing people to modify their actions.

When cultural institutions and values do not seem to change, this may reflect the weakness of the stimuli rather than their immovability. They are in any case capable of displaying more than one face, according to circumstance, as was shown by Albert Hirschman (1985) with respect to the extended family. Whereas Western commentators for a long time regarded extended families as depressing thrift and effort, many in the Third World knew better and accepted them as low-cost cooperative forms of the firm.

The primary trick in bringing about growth thus arguably lay outside either resource constraints or cultural rigidity. It lay in the removal of political disincentives. This is different from growth brought about by the positive institutional creations of the state: at least in modern times, the speed of the market response to the lifting of restraints de-emphasizes the importance of detailed debate about policy mixes.

Such debate goes on, endlessly, but it does not necessarily tell us much about what causes growth, only about its form and who stands to win or lose from it. These are noteworthy but secondary, almost derivative, matters. Possible support for this opinion is to be found in the astounding rates of growth achieved during the 1980s in mainland China, in a number of the large coastal provinces such as Guangdong and Jiangsu, right from the moment that restrictions on market activity were lifted. Barring accidents, we may expect to see a further spread of *intensive* growth to countries that do not impede its emergence. This spread could be faster than ever because of developments in a proximate cause of change, the transfer of advanced technologies and management techniques. As Peter Drucker (1987) observes, these things have been and can be taught.

The Role of the State

We may be able to throw some light on whether the centralized provision of public goods was indispensable for *intensive* growth by considering whether an effective state is a necessary condition for the presence of operating markets. A brace of tentative examples suggests not. While they do not prove that *intensive* growth would automatically follow without centralized provision, they do caution against assuming that it would not. With better examples it would be useful to distinguish between freely operating and expanding product markets on the one hand and markets in factors of production on the other. What is probably crucial is the removal of command interferences, especially in factor markets. It is political intervention by the command sector that most requires political surgery and factor markets that most need to be flexible. The constraints of mere custom, on the other hand, look adamantine but are surprisingly responsive to economic incentives or disincentives. This could alter the most basic aspects of social behavior. Sir Henry Maine pointed out that both the Spartan and the Venetian aristocracies—the latter as recently as the early eighteenth century A.D.—responded to the taxing of separate households, which were deemed to come into being with separate marriages, by turning to the polyandry of brothers. In other words, brothers shared a wife and saved on tax (Maine 1883, 124). How much more responsive can custom become?

The particular cases to which we may refer where governmental provision was absent or weak relate, first, to the spontaneously crime-free trade of Dobbo in the Aru Islands, Indonesia, during the nineteenth century. "It puts strange thoughts into one's head," wrote Alfred Russel Wallace (1962, 336), "about the mountain-load of government under which people exist in Europe" and, though requiring more investigation, seems to confirm that commerce was possible without governmental provision of law and order. Second, Gellner (1988, 233) refers to the "astonishing" case of the Lebanon, where the level of production and economic activity remained greater, at least for some time, than in many developing societies with "relatively effective" states. (We should point out that the states in many developing countries are probably not as strong as Gellner implies. Especially in Africa, they are facades for patrimonial regimes—see Jackson [1987].) There may be an asymmetry. On the one hand, a collapse of the state may, but need not, lead to a collapse of the economy, while on the other hand, there may be little chance of thriving economic activity where no functioning state has ever existed. Even so, the case of Dobbo challenges the indispensability of statehood, though perhaps only for small societies.

Historically, what happened was the unintended rather than deliberate dissolution of suppressants. Unintended consequences have always been a concern of the economist: here is another set. Rather than the moment of growth's inception—a fuzzy concept in a world with prior technical change and investment growth—being what was determined by the removal of suppressants, it was growth's form that was affected. Form and pace differed so much from country to country and rested so much on positive actions that they certainly do imply complex causes for growth. But this is a little illusory. The growth impulse was there, protean yet basic, waiting to be released. It was rather the form of each country's impediments, the political processes, and the diverse channels into which growth could run that were so complex.

Positive actions by government came only after the emergence of growth and rulers had learned that it was good. Some such measures had, of course, always been undertaken. Part of the task of kingship included building ever-normal granaries, unifying the coinage, and establishing courts of law. The *extensive* growth which was required to keep pace with the growth of population had itself often been accompanied by public investment. The aim was, however, seldom more than stabilization or expansion, retaining the existing hierarchies and customary levels of income. Rulers and ruling elites saw no merit in actions that might cause structural change. Why should they, when it must damage their own *relative* income position?

The conscious promotion of growth was thus not usual in the premodern state. At any rate, it was not primary. It followed rather than led. A government that undertook deliberate policies to encourage *intensive* growth would already be dismantling restrictions; or if market growth were occurring willy-nilly, the state would already have become too weak to maintain complete control over its subordinates.

The Bakufu—the central government—in late Tokugawa Japan is an illustration. The formidable stare on its face was belied by the reality in the provinces. Yoshihara (1986, 91) goes so far as to say of the provincial *han* administrative units that, "in a sense, Tokugawa Japan consisted of some 270 autonomous states." This decentralization would increase the number of a government's subjects who pressed it to favor growth, to remove what were seen as major remaining obstacles. A very interesting list of what these were in the eyes of a contemporary occurs in the writings of Honda Toshiaki (Keene 1969). The slow spiraling of change and complicated feedbacks, inscribed only on the handful of confetti which remains as documentary evidence, makes it hard to distinguish cause from effect. The Tokugawa Bakufu, when it found itself presiding over *intensive* growth, nevertheless did retain a degree of real power. The *han*s were not fully autonomous, there was some central economic policy. In the brutal circus of premodern politics, these nice but uncomprehended states of balance between collapsing constraints and acts of state, between central control and local development, could survive only fortuitously. That is why they were so rare.

Despite Perry Anderson's remark (1974b, 404) that precapitalist social formations were more various than those of capitalism, they had in common strikingly unequal distributions of wealth, income, and power. In the modern Western world, power may flow from wealth; in the premodern world, wealth flowed from power. Premodern politics were redistributive, but redistributive upward. For all the variety of political institutions, which does make the evolution of each unit a tangled tale, premodern history was very much *plus ça change, plus c'est la même chose.*

The difficulties of raising average income because of initially weak technologies, feeble institutions, and environments of high natural risk were real. It is not the intention to discount them. There was added, however, a more central disability: political power based on unchecked violence or the unconstrained threat of violence, which raised the social risks facing the entrepreneur. High and arbitrary taxation, even confiscation, was a powerful disincentive and the probability of penalties for conspicuous success even more so. Agreed, not everyone was dissuaded from taking up the profession of "mere merchant"—the Tudor phrase for him who specialized in trade without engaging in production. Certainly there were merchants, very skilled ones, yet the total volume of commercial activity was low, particularly in the bulk carriage of utilitarian goods. Merchants existed and could be rich but they were socially and politically marginalized in most warrior societies, indeed they were often communities of outlanders. They remained peculiarly vulnerable to arbitrary treatment. The producers of manufactures were more vulnerable still. They had at risk premises, stocks of raw materials, finished goods, coin and personal wealth.

Characteristic premodern political behavior was rent-seeking or pie-slicing, congealed though this might be into apparently static forms. The ruler and elite took by force or the threat of force a far bigger share of the social product than they contributed. The rules of government given to his son by a reportedly benevolent king of Kashmir included the injunction never to allow villagers to retain more food than they needed for one year plus the seed for the next harvest, lest they "become in a single year very formidable . . . strong enough to neglect the commands of the king" (Singh 1968, 39). The founder of the Tokugawa dynasty, Ieyasu, certainly set out with the intention that the peasants should "neither live nor die" (Kunio 1986, 92). Taxation unaccompanied by any significant return in services was the norm. Most tax was levied from the peasantry but its frequent revolts failed to force a lasting change.

The very rarity of the occasions when productive forces bore a heavy crop of fruit shows that the circumstances had to be privileged. The precise politics that let growth filter up are not yet clear. Essentially what happened was that power blocs came to cancel one another out while retaining the appearance of solidity. Ruler and nobility had to neutralize one another for enough investment income to be left in the hands of producers. We cannot specify the shares involved, or measure them given the sources that survive, but it is obvious that this was a straight and narrow passage. Normally those with nonmarket power—ruler and elite—either fell out so drastically, or were invaded by their peers from elsewhere, that the impulses toward *intensive* growth were checked again.

The Patterns of Growth

Scholars will eventually find more cases which were successful for a time. Yet in the circumstances it is hardly surprising that we know of few noteworthy ones, among which, to repeat, Song China, Tokugawa Japan, and early modern Europe are outstanding. From the time of the collapse of the Song, most of mainland Asia and the Near and Middle East were ruled by the Mongols. After their retreat there was a pause, but soon conquest regimes of similarly paralyzing selfishness once more took over the main societies: the Ottomans, the Mughals, the Manchu. All suppressed or failed to tolerate *intensive* growth. Invasions by warrior hordes bent on creating exploitative empires are more definitely negative forces than the myriad possible innovations of the Industrial Revolution period are positive ones.

In early modern times it was some of the peripheral societies of Eurasia that underwent transitions to *intensive* growth. In them, unusual political circumstances let markets expand, entrepreneurs prosper, and growth filter up. It helped that by then enough technical knowledge had accumulated to magnify the process and keep it going. Finally, states themselves learned the advantages of assisting growth. Something of this kind happened not only in Europe but as part of the rebirth of *intensive* growth in East Asia, led this time by Japan rather than China. The world did not have to wait for a single-country industrial revolution to taste the fruits of *intensive* growth.

Notes

1. See McCormack (1988, 3–4).
2. Maddison (1982) makes clear the sequence of changes in world economic leadership.
3. There is a clever argument for the independent role of spatial arrangements in social change in Dodgshon (1987), but this does not refer directly to configurations of natural resources.

Chapter 6

Civilizing and Decivilizing Processes

Stephen Mennell

For most of the twentieth century, as I noted in the Introduction, historians and social scientists have tended to steer clear of investigating long-term social processes in general. But they have given a particularly wide berth to a set of questions which preoccupied their nineteenth-century precursors: the issue of how what may loosely be called humans' "psychological" makeup changes in the course of social development. The problem is often raised only to be summarily dismissed. In a recent elementary textbook (1994), Chirot, for example, poses the question:

> why, despite the essential psychological and biological similarity of humans today and those of, say, twenty thousand years ago, almost all aspects of our lives except for our basic physical functions are so different, and why, despite the basic similarity of all human beings on earth today (we are all one species and interbreed perfectly well) there are such huge differences in economic, social and political behaviour. (Chirot 1994, *xvi*)

Much rests on the word "essential"—it obscures the obvious point that some aspects of human psychology change little if at all, while others are plainly greatly changed by changing social context. Sociologists now fashionably use the jargon-word "habitus" to denote those changeable features. Its meaning is not very different from *mentalités,* as used by the Annales historians, but it is more exactly described by the everyday expression "second nature."[1] It refers to those layers of our personality makeup which are not inherent or innate but are very deeply *habituated* in us by learning through social experience from birth onward—so deeply habituated, in fact, that they feel "natural" or inherent even to ourselves.

Nineteenth-century social evolutionists tended to discuss these matters in the framework of unilinear evolutionary stages, from "savagery" through "barbarism" to "civilization." Members of industrial societies like themselves were the product of "progress," and had reached a state of being "civilized," with a clear implication of being better and superior. In chapter 1, Goudsblom has not only discussed the weaknesses of such unilinear (and value-laden) conceptions, but also suggested how the essential questions can now be posed and processual answers reached—through a combination of chronology and "phaseology"—avoiding the earlier weaknesses.

Such a reframing of the question of the connection between human behavior and long-term social development starts from the recognition that

> in order to survive in the ecological and social niches in which they find themselves, people have to acquire certain skills. A repertory of such skills may be called a regime. . . . Regimes give rise to a mixture of aptitudes and inaptitudes. Out of the virtually unlimited range of possible forms of conduct, people everywhere learn to realise a few. The skills and habits which help them to survive in one niche, be it in a royal court or a university, may be of no value or even detrimental in other niches. (Goudsblom 1994, 15–16)[2]

Following Norbert Elias, Goudsblom suggests that the formation and transmission of such regimes be called "civilizing processes," and these processes generate trained incapacities as well as capacities. In his book *Fire and Civilization* (1992b) and in chapters 2 and 3, Goudsblom has applied these ideas to the formation of regimes in two major ecological transitions—the fire and agrarian "revolutions"—in the history of humanity as a whole.

In the present chapter, I want to return to Norbert Elias's original theory, presented in his classic *The Civilizing Process* (originally published in German in 1939 but known widely only in more recent years and only in 1994 published in a single English volume for the first time), and also to draw on later elaborations and extensions of the theory by Elias and others in the research tradition he initiated. The theory presents a complex skein of ideas about state formation, violence, culture, personality, and overall processes of social development which together represent one of the richest and most exciting (and still relatively unquarried) sources of inspiration for further comparative-historical research. This chapter will serve as background for the next, in which I want to raise in a very preliminary and programmatic way a potentially important extension—and by implication a test—of Elias's theory of civilizing processes, by looking for processes in the history of China, India, and Japan comparable with those described by Elias in Europe. In order to explain why I think this is important and interesting, I will first give a brief summary of Elias's theory of civilizing processes, and indicate the main controversies which have surrounded his work.

Civilizing Processes: A Brief Outline of the Theory

The basic idea of *The Civilizing Process* is that there is a link between the long-term structural development of societies and changes in people's social character, typical personality makeup, or habitus. The first of the two original volumes deals with changes in manners and modes of feeling in Western Europe from the late Middle Ages to the Victorian period, while the second presents a detailed study of the process of state formation, again in Europe, since the Dark Ages. As the structure of societies becomes more complex, manners, culture, and personality also change in a particular and discernible direction, first among elite groups, then gradually more widely:

> if in a particular region, the power of central authority grows, if over a larger or smaller area people are *forced* to live at peace with one another, the moulding of affects and the standards of the demands made upon emotional management are very gradually changed as well. (Elias 1994, 165; my emphasis and modification to published translation.)

Elias's theory of state formation implicitly begins from Max Weber's definition of the state as an organization which successfully upholds a claim to binding rule making over a territory, by virtue of commanding a monopoly of the legitimate use of violence (Weber 1978 [1922], 1: 54), but he bypasses the problematic red herring of "legitimacy" by linking a rising level of internal security and calculability in everyday life directly to the formation of habitus. He is more interested than Weber in the *process* through which a monopoly of the means of violence (*and* taxation) is established and extended. After discussing the period of the early European Middle Ages, during which centrifugal forces were dominant in the process of feudalization, resulting in the extreme fragmentation of territory and of effective rule (1994, 273–334), Elias outlines the processes at work during the subsequent period when centripetal forces, fluctuatingly and with regressions, gradually regained the upper hand—much earlier in the territories that were to become England and France than in those that were to become Germany and Italy. A particularly vivid feature of his theory of state formation is his model of the "elimination contest" between numerous rival territorial magnates, a violent competitive process with a compelling sequential dynamic through which successively larger territorial units emerge with more effective central monopoly apparatuses. Elias's account of state formation in Europe emphasizes the initially relatively small disparities between many small territories, and subsequently the relatively even, though fluctuating, balances between contending elements within the emerging states. These were ideal conditions for the operation of the "monopoly mechanism" (the development of more effective central monopolies of the means of violence and taxation) and the "royal mechanism" (the accretion of power to kings through their ability to "play off" relatively equally balanced social interests against each other).

State formation is only one process interweaving with others to enmesh individuals in increasingly complex webs of interdependence. It interweaves with the division of labor, the growth of trade and towns, the use of money, and increasing population, in a spiral process. Internal pacification of territory facilitates trade, which facilitates the growth of towns and division of labor and generates taxes which support larger administrative and military organizations, which in turn facilitate the internal pacification of larger territories, and so on—a cumulative process experienced as a compelling force by people caught up in it. Furthermore, according to Elias, the gradually higher standards of habitual self-restraint engendered in people contribute in turn to the upward spiral—being necessary, for example, to the formation of gradually more effective and calculable administration. Elias is not seeking single causal factor explanations, but tracing how various causal strands interweave over time to produce an overall process with increasing momentum: his model of explanation is a "process model" (Mennell 1989a, 177 ff) which reveals not "structure *and* process" but the structure *of* processes.

Thus Elias by no means denies the importance of economic strands in long-term social development, but he particularly emphasizes the significance of control over the means of violence and denies that these can be *reduced* to economic processes (in this he anticipated such neo-Weberians as Mann 1986, 1993). Elias suggests that sociologists have paid insufficient attention to the *taming of warriors* as a necessary process in social development generally. *The Civilizing Process* shows some of the stages in the "courtization" of a minority of the old European warrior aristocracy—their transformation from the end of the Middle Ages into a class of *courtiers*—while in *The Court Society* (1983) he shows how this process found expression in many facets of courtly culture toward the end of the *ancien régime:* aristocratic romanticism, French classical drama, the formal gardens of Le Nôtre, and the Western epistemological tradition of *homo clausus,* among other things.

If violence is so central to Elias's underlying problematic, why does *The Civilizing Process* begin by looking at those famous instances of disgusting medieval manners, and the development of conventions about eating, washing, spitting, blowing one's nose, urinating and defecating, undressing? He focused particularly on these most basic, "natural" or "animalic" of human functions because these are activities human beings cannot biologically avoid no matter what society, culture, or age they live in. Moreover, infants are born in the same emotional condition everywhere, so that the *lifetime* point of departure is always the same. Therefore if change occurs in the way these functions are handled, it can be seen rather clearly. But his underlying concern is with topics more central to the interests of most comparative-historical sociologists: violence and aggressiveness. In Europe, at least, these became more tamed and more hidden behind the scenes of social life along with defecation, nakedness, and the rest. There is also, through gradual changes in the socialization process over the generations, a concomitant hiding of these matters in the unconscious, behind the scenes of *mental* life.

Elias speaks of civilizing processes on three levels:[3]

1.The individual level. Infants and children have to acquire through learning the adult standards of behavior and feeling prevalent in their society; to speak of this as a civilizing process is more or less to use another term for "socialization," and that this process has a typical structure and sequence is not disputed. Researchers from Freud and Piaget onward have debated the details of the sequence of childhood development, but few would now question that there *is* a sequence.

2. The level of particular societies. The second level is more controversial. Where did these standards come from? They have not always existed, nor always been the same. Central to Elias's argument is
the contention that it is possible to identify long-term civilizing processes in the shaping of standards of behavior and feeling over many
generations within particular cultures. That these standards *change* is
not disputed; what generates controversy is the proposition that the
changes take the form of *structured processes* of change with a discernible—though unplanned—*direction* over time.

Lest there be any misunderstanding, let me explicitly draw attention
to a linguistic problem. The word *direction* has two meanings. It can
convey the sense of conscious and intentional management and steering of affairs, as in a phrase like "under government direction." That is
not at all what I mean here by "the problem of direction"—we are
concerned with blind processes which are not the outcome of the plans
and intentions of any particular individual people, but are the unintended product of the interweaving of many people's plans and intentions. Such "undirected" interweaving can give rise to processes which
have direction in a sense more akin to the physicists' concepts of
"vector" and "momentum" (Mennell 1992).

Elias argues that as webs of interdependence become denser and
more extensive, there gradually takes place a shift in the *balance* between external constraints (*Fremdzwänge*—constraints *by other people*) and self-constraints (*Selbstzwänge*), in favor of the latter. His book
on time and timing (1992) brings out particularly clearly the link between social and personality changes arising from the necessity of
coordinating more and more complicated sequences of activities, and
implies (if it does not explicitly state) that this link should hold in all
cultures. The pressures on individuals to exercise greater *foresight* take
various forms: Elias discusses especially the processes of rationalization and "psychologization," and the advance of thresholds of shame
and embarrassment.

Psychologization is linked to the idea that spreading webs of interdependence tend to be associated with *relatively* more equal power
ratios and "functional democratization," meaning more and more re-
ciprocal controls between more and more social groups. Less ab-
stractly: "More people are forced more often to pay more attention to
more other people" (Goudsblom 1989, 722). This produces pressures
toward greater consideration of the consequences of one's own actions

for other people on whom one is more or less dependent, and there tends in consequence to be an increase in "mutual identification." This idea is not new to Elias—it was expressed very clearly by Alexis de Tocqueville[4]—but it has a very direct bearing on matters of violence and cruelty. The *advance of thresholds of shame and embarrassment* also involves increased foresight, in the sense of greater vigilance in anticipating social dangers, especially the transgression of various social prohibitions.

Rationalization, Elias stresses, has no absolute beginning in human history. Just as there was no point at which human beings suddenly began to possess a "conscience," there is none before which they were completely "irrational." Still more misleading is it to think of rationality as some kind of property of individual minds in isolation from each other. "There is no such thing as 'reason,' only at most 'rationalization' " (Elias 1994, 480). What actually changes is the way people are bonded with each other in society, and in consequence the molding of personality structure. Elias's argument is that the forms of behavior we call "rationality" are produced within a social figuration in which extensive transformation of external compulsions into internal compulsions takes place:

> The complementary concepts of "rationality" and "irrationality" refer to the relative parts played by short-term affects and long-term conceptual models of observable reality in individual behavior. The greater the importance of the latter in the delicate balance between affective and reality-oriented commands, the more "rational" is behavior. (Elias 1983, 92)

By extension, Elias contends that "rational understanding" is not the motor of the "civilizing" of ... behavior" (1994, 95), thus arguing against those who would wish to enlist Weber in support of viewing rationalization as the great propellant of long-term social development.

3. *The level of humanity as a whole.* This third level brings us back to the sorts of questions posed by the social evolutionists of the Victorian era. Particularly in his later works (1987a, 1991, 1992), Elias himself became increasingly preoccupied with very long-term processes in the development of human society as a whole. No civilizing process in any particular human group, it must be remembered, represents an absolute beginning. It never proceeds *in vacuo,* without reference to other—earlier or contemporary—civilizing processes undergone by other human groups. Jerry Bentley, in his book *Old World Encounters* (1993), reminds us that from ancient times the people of Asia, Europe, and Africa were constantly encountering and intermingling with each other, powerfully promoting change, fostering the spread of technologies, ideas, beliefs, values, and religions. Just as every individual lifetime civilizing process is a part of a longer-term development in a particular society, so also are civilizing processes in every society parts of still longer-term civilizing processes which encompass humanity as a whole. In this even longer-term perspective, humanity as a whole has undergone a collective learning process in which it has acquired such distinctively human skills as speech, the use of fire, the making of tools and weapons from wood, stone, and metals, and the vast and still growing stock of subsequent knowledge.[5]

Many people involved in the study of long-term developmental processes will be able to adjust to a notion of "civilizing process" used in a technical sense for a collective learning process, at least if it is confined to matters such as technology and the scale of social organization. (That means when it is used in a sense related to the traditional use of terms like "ancient civilizations.") Many will have more difficulty in accepting that it can also apply to changes in an identifiable direction taking place in matters of culture and habitus. This reservation goes back to the time-honored dichotomy between "civilization" and "culture" as expounded by Alfred Weber (1935), introduced into American sociology by Robert MacIver, and resuscitated by Hans-Peter Duerr in his critique of Elias's theory, *Der Mythos vom Zivilisationsprozesse* (1988, 1990, 1993).[6] Major debates have developed in consequence about Elias's theory, and two of the key issues center on the continuing incidence of violence in human society and on the possibility of discerning in other major world historic cultures processes comparable to the European civilizing process described by Elias.[7] The former I shall now discuss in this chapter, the latter in the next.

Decivilizing Processes and the Problem of Violence

It is a serious misreading of the theory of civilizing processes to see it as a model of "progress," let alone *inevitable* progress.[8] On the contrary, the process of internal pacification of territory was a highly contingent and precarious one. The means of violence continue to play a part even in the most internally pacified society, even though—like defecation, urination, nakedness, and other aspects of manners—they may over time come to be increasingly hidden behind the scenes of social life. They may, literally and figuratively, be confined to barracks; but they are still there. The gradually established social control of dangers was a precondition for the more "civilized" standard of conduct, but

> The armour of civilized conduct would crumble very rapidly if, through a change in society, the degree of insecurity that existed earlier were to break in upon us again, and if danger became as incalculable as once it was. Corresponding fears would burst the limits set to them today. (Elias 1994, 253*n*).

In other words, civilized conduct takes a long time to construct, but remains contingent upon the maintenance of a high level of internal pacification, and can be destroyed rather quickly. There is a certain asymmetry between civilizing and decivilizing processes: the former can only be relatively long-term processes, while the latter can gain ascendancy relatively rapidly. We need to think in terms of a tension-balance between conflicting pressures. It could be argued that decivilizing trends, or decivilizing pressures, are *always* present. Indeed, civilizing processes arise (as blind, unplanned processes) out of people's struggles to solve the problems posed to them in their lives by decivilizing pressures—for example, the threat of violence and insecurity. So we need to think of civilizing and decivilizing pressures as pushing against each other. The question is which forces gain the upper hand, in the short term or the long term.

If the curbing of affects, including impulses toward the use of violence, is contingent on internal pacification *within* the territory of emerging state-societies, the use of violence *between* states (that is, *war*) showed few signs of diminishing. The release of the affects in battle—the sheer enjoyment of fighting (*Angriffslust*) which had been evident among early medieval warriors—had perhaps become a little curbed; but that had been offset by the increasing scale of warfare as, over the centuries, battles between territorially larger states had come to be fought out by larger numbers of people over larger geographical spaces. This trend continued into and through the twentieth century;

that is the significance of our referring to the two major conflicts as *world* wars. Ironically, the nuclear standoff between the two super-powers in the decades after the Second World War was one of *relative* stability. Godfried van Benthem van den Bergh (1992), employing aspects of the theory of civilizing processes, has convincingly argued that the morally repulsive strategy of Mutually Assured Destruction (MAD) provided a powerful external constraint toward self-constraint on the part of the superpowers, and on many of their clients in more local conflicts across the globe. In the absence of any worldwide "or-ganization which successfully upholds a claim to binding rule-making over a territory, by virtue of commanding a monopoly of the legitimate use of violence" (Max Weber 1992: I, 54), MAD in effect served as a functional alternative to a nonexistent world government. Toward the end of that period, it became fashionable to speak of the incipient "globalization" of world society (Albrow and King 1990; Mennell 1990b; Kilminster, forthcoming 1996), and indeed the long-term ef-fects of the globalization of markets (among other things) are difficult to foresee in detail but are likely to be very great. Yet, after the brief euphoria of 1989–90, when both a "new world order" and "the end of history" (Fukuyama 1992) were proclaimed, wars and ethnic conflicts appear to be breaking out widely. Indeed, some territorial units which appeared relatively peaceful—Yugoslavia, the USSR—have dissolved into strife, as less inclusive we-identities such as Croat, Serb, Bosnian, or Chechen have risen to dominance and, apparently, "mutual identifi-cation" has diminished. Recent history, which may indeed be too re-cent to be brought fully into focus in a book concerned with very long-term history, serves at least as a reminder that the balances be-tween civilizing and decivilizing pressures, and between centripetal and centrifugal forces, still continue to fluctuate.

In struggles between members of different "survival units" (tribes or, later, states) there is, historically speaking, nothing very unusual about the mass murder of defeated enemies, or about pogroms of out-sider groups. They were long taken for granted. In Europe, however, there had gradually emerged a system of states which, in world per-spective, were territorially relatively small but also relatively effective (a point which Eric Jones also stresses in accounting for the "European miracle" of economic growth). Even there, only gradually in the course of state-formation processes did outbreaks of violence and cruelty by one social group toward another diminish in frequency and ruthlessness. As we have seen, according to Elias, that they did so at all was because the spreading webs of interdependence associated with state formation and other long-term developmental processes tend to be associated with relatively more equal power ratios and functional democratization.

On the other hand, the pressures inherent in the process of functional democratization which tend toward increasing the level of mutual identification are never sufficient altogether to eradicate conflicts between groups within the same state-society. Indeed, these same processes of differentiation create problems of coordination. Larger-scale organization in state and economy forces groups of people together in closer interdependencies than formerly; and these new patterns create new concentrations of power resources, new inequalities, new opportunities for intergroup struggles. All the same, if these struggles take place *within* a relatively effective state, we would generally expect a high probability of them most often being pursued by nonviolent means.

That it is only a probability; however, many instances of large-scale violence within state-societies serve as reminders. Of all of them, the genocides of the Nazi period have caused the greatest affront to Europeans' image of themselves as "civilized," precisely because they took place within the framework of that system of relatively small and effective state-societies characteristic of the continent. People still find it difficult to understand in a relatively detached way how such a catastrophic, albeit relatively brief, decivilizing episode could have happened in Europe.

Civilizing processes involve a change in the balance between external constraints (*Fremdzwänge,* constraints by *other people*) and self-constraints (*Selbstzwänge*)—the balance tilting toward the latter in the control of behavior in the average person. Decivilizing processes may be defined as a tilting of the balance back in favor of external constraints. But in neither case will the operation of self-constraints remain unchanged if changes take place in the patterning of external constraints—the behavior of other people. Calculation of the external constraints always plays a part in the steering of conduct, and if the calculations suddenly or gradually yield different outcomes, behavior will change.

Still more will it change if the outcomes become—as Elias said in the remark quoted above—more incalculable: the pattern of people's fears responds to changes in the dangers they face. And one of the distinguishing characteristics of decivilizing trends is a rise in the level of danger and a fall in its calculability.

During times of social crisis—military defeats, political revolutions, rampant inflation, soaring unemployment, separately or, as happened in Germany after the First World War, in rapid sequence—fears rise because control of social events has declined. Rising fears make it still more difficult to control events. That makes people still more susceptible to wish fantasies about means of alleviating the situation. A vicious circle or "double-bind process" is set up, and a process of that kind can be clearly seen in Germany after 1918, helping to explain the rise of the Nazis and the appeal of racial beliefs—one instance of the more general category of "fantasy-laden" beliefs.[9] The Weimar period plainly provided fertile soil for such beliefs. Elias (1996, 171–203, 214–23) himself wrote about the decline of the state's monopoly of violence under the Weimar Republic, and Jonathan Fletcher (1995) has argued that it was then, rather than subsequently under the Nazi regime, that decivilizing forces were most clearly dominant. The grim paradox is that it was the return to a highly effective state monopolization of the means of violence (though somewhat less "behind the scenes" than formerly) under Hitler, together with the renewed dangers and fears provided by the Second World War, that permitted the Holocaust to be so effectively organized.

It is striking how hard the Nazi regime had to strive to diminish the identification which many Germans felt with their fellow Germans, the Jews (which was evident, for instance, in the popular reaction to *Kristallnacht* in 1938). It was not merely a matter of propaganda, whipping up a sense of danger. The Jews were first removed to ghettos, breaking their personal contacts with their non-Jewish neighbors. Then, under the official pretext of "resettlement in the east," they were removed to transit camps, labor camps, and finally extermination camps "behind the scenes" (*to some extent*) at least of metropolitan Germany. The regime remained apprehensive of German public opinion even at this stage (on all this, see Noakes and Pridham 1988, 3: 997–1208). "Mutual identification" was apparently not negligible, but it was successfully bypassed. Its bypassing, as well as the mass murders themselves and all the innumerable actions of lesser cruelty which led up to them, were triumphs of rational organization. Modern social organization vastly multiplied the technical capacity to kill.

Are There Long-Term Decivilizing Processes?

There are good reasons to think that decivilizing spurts may operate more quickly and dramatically than civilizing processes. Rising levels of danger and incalculability in social life quite quickly render people more susceptible to fears and fantasies. In addition, it must be remembered that, though standards change from generation to generation in the course of a social learning process extending over many lifetimes, the prevalent standards of controls at any point in the process have to be acquired—or not acquired—by every individual in every generation through an individual learning process, by definition no longer than an individual lifetime. Abrupt changes in social circumstances may seriously disrupt the continuity of socialization.

Yet it is interesting to ask whether there have also been long-term decivilizing processes, *structured* processes of change extending over several generations. When civilizing pressures are dominant, the direction of change is toward the formation of social standards which require a more demanding level of habitual self-constraint by people in each successive generation. Are there any well-documented cases of decivilizing pressures dominating in such a way that, rather than abrupt change in response to sudden events, from one generation to the next the social standards of habitual self-constraint become *less* demanding? To observe such a case, one would really need to observe changes over a minimum of three generations. Loïc Wacquant (1992) has suggested that the black ghettos of the United States in the twentieth century provide a clear instance of just such an intergenerational process.

On a larger scale, perhaps the most obvious place to look for signs of longer-term decivilizing processes would be in the context of the more or less total collapse of complex societies. The instance best known and most discussed among Western historians and social scientists is the collapse of the Roman empire. The archaeologist Joseph Tainter (1988) gives a surprisingly long list of other examples. They include the Western Chou empire in China, the Mesopotamian empires, the Egyptian Old Kingdom, the Hittite empire, the Minoan civilization, and several of the pre-Columbian New World empires.

The most significant questions that may be asked about these longer-term decivilizing processes fall into two main groups. The first group of questions are "structural": in what circumstances do the chains of interdependence in society begin to break, and thus why do levels of complexity, differentiation, and integration start to decline? The second group concerns the outcome of such processes of structural unraveling for people's experience: what are the cultural and psychological consequences and the impact on people's day-to-day conduct?[10]

Tainter provides a careful eleven-fold categorization and critique of earlier explanations of social collapse. His own favored explanation is essentially economic. Collapse comes about because "investment in socio-political complexity often reaches a point of declining marginal returns" (1988, 118). By returns he means "benefits to people"—by implication mainly powerful elite groups—and investment covers expenditure on legitimation activities or alternatively the means of coercion as well as on more narrowly economic infrastructure. The main weakness of Tainter's theory, however, is that he has difficulty in specifying the point at which diminishing returns set in—independently, that is, of collapse itself. The theory, therefore, has a somewhat *ex post facto* quality.

In fact, we seem to have no general theory of structural collapse, and perhaps it is not sensible to look for one. The precipitating circumstances are possibly too varied to be effectively subsumed under a higher-level abstraction like "diminishing marginal returns." The chances of fruitful generalization may perhaps be greater in relation to my second group of questions, concerning the cultural and psychological effects and the impact on people's conduct when "structural unraveling" occurs in various forms and degrees.

It seems probable that an increase in levels of danger and incalculability, and a decline in the capacity of central monopoly apparatuses to enforce their authority, will be associated with the re-emergence of free-rider problems. The consequence will be the onset of disinvestment in collective goods. Individual people and small groups simply find it less safe than it formerly was to depend on other people located at a great distance down social chains whose links are beginning to break. Collective arrangements which ultimately rested on the capacity of authorities to enforce them can no longer be relied upon. In the space of a generation or two, smaller and less dense webs of interdependence entailing fewer pressures toward foresight in the coordination of activities may, through the socialization process, result in diminution of these capacities. People need to practice them if they are to be able to call on them at will. Conversely, in situations of greater insecurity, learning aptitudes resting on a very different temperament may have greater survival value. Thus, when social circumstances (or niches) change, even if civilized self-constraints are not lost rapidly, over a period of time we would expect a kind of social selection of a new range of aptitudes. These changes of regime may be in what we have defined as a decivilizing direction—as, for example, when the regime of the warrior once more becomes of greater survival value than that of the democratic politician.

In studying the psychological and cultural components of this process in historical contexts such as the decline of Rome, contemporary studies of the effects of increased levels of violence on adults and children in places like Northern Ireland and Lebanon (Cairns and Wilson 1985; Hosin 1983) ought to be relevant. Increased levels of danger ought to be associated with increased fear and anxiety, and with a lessening of controls. As always, in practice it is not easy to make inferences from short-term studies to long-term trends. The increase in anxiety shows up in Northern Ireland, but as realistic, not neurotic, anxiety. On the other hand, it may be thought that the relatively high level of intercommunal conflict in Northern Ireland over many generations is reflected in the rather high fantasy content of popular beliefs in the province (see MacDonald 1983). But applying such insights to historical evidence is quite difficult, in part because periods of social disintegration are times when documentary evidence is likely to be less complete and clear.

Notes

1. This point was made in conversation by Norbert Elias.

2. On the usefulness of the notion of "regime" in the study of world history, see also Fred Spier, "Regimes as Structuring Principles for Big History" (1995).

3. The distinction is explained most clearly by Goudsblom (1984); see also Mennell (1989a, 200–24).

4. Tocqueville cites Mme de Sévigné's jocular comments on people being broken on the wheel after the tax riots in Rennes in 1675 as an instance of the lack of feeling of members of one social class for the sufferings of members of another, and speaks of the subsequent "softening of manners as social conditions become more equal" (Alexis de Tocqueville, *Democracy in America*, pt. 2, bk. 3, chap. 1, quoted in Stone and Mennell 1980, 102–6).

5. As already mentioned, Goudsblom's work on the domestication of fire (1992) and in chapters 2 and 3 above proceeds on this third level, and it could be argued that Eric Jones's focus is also on processes at the level of humanity as a whole.

6. See the countercritique of Duerr by Goudsblom and myself (forthcoming 1996).

7. Other debates about Elias's work include whether comparable patterns of "civilized" conduct can emerge in stateless societies, thus refuting or severely qualifying the link Elias stresses with the monopolization of violence by state apparatuses; whether there has been a significant upturn in violence in recent decades in Western societies, thus qualifying the link Elias makes with lengthening chains of interdependence; and whether the so-called "permissive society" represents a reversal of the historic trend in European societies. For a discussion of these, see Mennell (1989a, 1990a).

8. See Elias's discussion of "the problem of the 'inevitability' of social development" in chapter 6 of *What is Sociology?* (1978, 158–74), and also Philip Abrams's appreciation of Elias's solution to the problem (Abrams 1982 145–46).

9. This paragraph needs to be understood in the context of Elias's theory of knowledge and of "involvement and detachment"; see Elias (1987) and Mennell (1989a, 158–99).

10. A third set of questions should not be overlooked: whether the possible loss of certain learned psychological qualities and behavioral capacities—for example, any tilting of the balance back away from self-constraints, any associated decline in the general capacity for detour behavior and the exercise of foresight, and any decline in the breadth of mutual identification—may contribute to structural decline once it has started.

——— Chapter 7 ———

Asia and Europe: Comparing Civilizing Processes

Stephen Mennell

Can long-term processes comparable with those described by Elias for Europe be found in other historic cultures of the world? The question is an important and challenging one. It can be used to reorient the way we look at the development of non-European historic cultures, both in guiding new research and in reassessing already familiar historical evidence. Such research can also serve as a major test of the basic sociological propositions underpinning Elias's theory. It is likely that in consequence the original theory will be qualified and amended, but also extended and refined. Given the scope of the theory of civilizing processes, any refinement and extension will potentially be of great value in increasing our understanding of long-term processes of social development generally.

The task has only recently been taken up by a few scholars,[1] and what follows is a mainly programmatic exploration of the problems involved in such a potentially vast research project.

Seeking Evidence

For purposes of this preliminary exploration of the problem of whether Elias's theory can usefully be extended to the study of Asian history, the many component part-processes of the overall model of civilizing processes can be roughly grouped under five headings: (1) state formation and allied processes; (2) taming of warriors and courtization; (3) changes in manners and forms of cultural expression; (4) psychogenetic changes, or changes in habitus; and (5) science and knowledge.

State Formation and Allied Processes

Probably the easiest component of Elias's overall theory for which to find parallels in Asia is state-formation processes. China, Japan, and India have all witnessed cycles of integration and disintegration, state formation, and feudalization.[2] That alerts us to the need always to look out for, and to study the structure of, decivilizing as well as civilizing processes. But that is not so very different from Europe.

China presents a complicated picture. Even though it has existed as a recognizably continuous political unit for far longer than any European state (Elvin 1973), there have been long periods when centrifugal forces regained dominance over the centripetal, when the effectiveness of central authorities became much weaker than formerly, and when the level of danger and incalculability in everyday life over much of Chinese territory rose rather than fell. Even so, throughout the two millennia since the Han empire—contemporary with the Roman empire in Western Eurasia—China seems to have remained, in Benedict Anderson's (1983) phrase, an "imagined community." And some institutions, like the mandarin class and the examination system, survived with little break from about A.D. 700 in the T'ang era.

India's history is even more complicated by periods of fragmentation and invasion: after the early Mauryan and Gupta empires (325–150 B.C. and A.D. 320–540 respectively), which embraced large parts of the subcontinent, there followed a period of feudalization, followed in turn by Muslim hegemony in the north and the Vijayanga empire (1336–1646) in the south, which gradually disintegrated. Then there came the great period of the Mughal empire in the north (from A.D. 1526) and the Maratha empire to its south from the mid-seventeenth century, both of them decaying and being subordinated to rising British dominance in the late eighteenth and early nineteenth centuries.

Japanese history is often seen as more easily comparable with Europe's. But there, too, there were at least two separate phases of state formation, which the continuity in the office of emperor very superficially disguises.[3] In the Nara period (from A.D. 645) there was a centralized administration modeled on that of the T'ang empire, and at Kyoto there emerged a humane, aesthetic court society with a distinctly softening influence. But from the late eleventh century, military clans arose, with feudalization and fragmentation associated with tax-free estates, especially those of the armed Buddhist monasteries. For most of the Ashikaga period (1339–1573) there were full-scale civil wars, and an almost total fragmentation and breakdown of the old houses and class system. Only in the last quarter of the sixteenth century, the period of the "three unifiers," did integration regain the upper hand, leading to the establishment of stable centralized rule by the Tokugawa shogunate based at Tokyo in 1603.

This points to an important, if obvious, methodological rule in the comparative study of civilizing processes: what is to be compared is *the structure of underlying social processes.* The relevant comparisons may therefore be between Western Europe, China, Japan, or India at quite different periods of chronological time.

For example, the period in Chinese history which most closely corresponds to the stage in Western European state formation that Elias calls the "elimination contest" was that of the Warring States (ca. 400–221 B.C.)—all of a millennium and a half earlier than the corresponding phase in Europe. Later, the period of the Song emperors (A.D. 960–1279) is sometimes referred to as China's "early modern" period, when it attained the self-sustained intensive growth which, in early modern Europe, was the context for the civilizing processes described by Elias.

In the case of Japan, the nearest equivalent to the "elimination contest" in Europe occurred in the late fifteenth and sixteenth centuries (sometimes referred to by analogy with China as Japan's "Warring States" period), leading up to the era of the three unifiers (1573–1600)—much later, and also briefer than the European one. But this was followed immediately by the Tokugawa era, Japan's own "early modern" period, which was nearly contemporaneous with the European one. Among other things, the late sixteenth century and early seventeenth century saw the reconstruction of the Japanese upper class from diverse elements, as in the Renaissance period in Europe. This leads me on to:

The Taming of Warriors and Courtization

As Goudsblom argues in chapter 3, domination by warriors appears to be a universal feature of the development of agrarian societies. By extension the "taming of warriors" is a constituent of any successful state-formation process—it is implied in the very idea of the formation of a monopoly of violence. Parallels abound in Asian history to what

Elias described in Europe. The fullest study to date is Eiko Ikegami's *The Taming of the Samurai* (1995). She traces the changing place of the samurai in Japanese society, from their rise in ancient Japan, through their dominance as warrior lords in the medieval period, to their formal abolition at the Meiji Restoration. An especially important phase was that of the three unifiers and the subsequent early Tokugawa period. A famous symptom of the processes at work here were the "Sword Hunts" of the late sixteenth century, when peasants were made to surrender their weapons to the government; the problem was on the one hand to restrict the means of violence to the samurai class as a means of controlling the rest of the population, then to control their use by the samurai independently of the state either against other social groups or in disputes among themselves.[4] Especially under the second and third shoguns of the Tokugawa period (Iemitsu and Tsunayoshi), there were explicit drives to "civilize" the warrior class, harnessing Confucianism to the purpose. Out of the turbulent beginning of the Tokugawa state, the solution that emerged was a transformation of the samurai into a class of vassal-bureaucrats. On the other hand, the *daimyo,* the local nobility of Japan, retained substantial autonomy in their domains (see Jones's remarks, page 97 above). In both respects they perhaps came to resemble Prussian Junkers more than the seventeenth- and eighteenth-century French nobility or English gentry. The balance of forces was such that the operation of a "royal mechanism" in the shogun's favor is not very evident, although later power ratios shifted as a large proportion of *daimyo* became indebted to the merchant class.

Ikegami portrays Japanese state-formation processes as proceeding along very different lines from those seen in Europe at the same time, but she perhaps slightly overemphasizes Japanese distinctiveness. She contends that the so-called "harmonious collective culture" of modern Japan is "paradoxically connected with a history of conflicts and struggles" (1995, 5). That is not much of a paradox in light of Elias's interpretation of the emergence of (relatively) democratic states in Europe.[5] But the balance of similarities and differences is largely a matter of the focus one chooses—the close-up or the view from afar.

If the taming of warriors is a necessary feature of successful state formation in agrarian societies, the process of courtization is more diverse and it is less easy to generalize confidently about its place in overall civilizing processes. Certainly there are many instances of courts as hotbeds of intrigue, as in the Chinese and Japanese imperial courts, and of courts as hothouses for luxury and rich cultural elaboration (including cuisine, for example, as well as the higher arts), as in the Mughal, Maratha, and Rajput courts of India (Patnaik 1985). The problem is how such courts related to the power ratios of the wider society. Japan illustrates the problem very well. From the defeat of the Taira by Minamoto Yoritomo in 1185, right through to the Meiji Restoration nearly 700 years later, there was a bifurcation between the imperial court, with courtiers and elaborate ceremonials but little power, and the shogun's bakufu ("camp-office"), headquarters of the most powerful warriors and effective government—located elsewhere, latterly more than two hundred miles away in Tokyo. For a time, there was even a double dualism, when the shogun too became a purely ceremonial figure, with real power in the hands of another powerful warrior. This is all very different from the court of Louis XIV, where, as Elias showed, in the hands of an absolutist monarch ceremonial was used as an instrument of power over the erstwhile warrior class.

This leads in turn to the question of how power struggles and state-formation processes in Asia are connected, if at all, to changes within the wider society in habitus, manners, and forms of cultural expression.

Changes in Manners and Forms of Cultural Expression

The period in European history when, according to Elias, standards of social conduct were set in motion and when in the words of Caxton's *Book of Curtesye* "thingis whilom used ben now leyd aside" (Elias 1994, 66) was one of relative social fluidity. New upper strata were being formed from elements of diverse origin, and social competition was strong. The situation is very different from the way the great Asian empires have long been perceived to have functioned. Since the early nineteenth century, the West has generally viewed the empires of Indian and Chinese history particularly through concepts like "Oriental despotism" in their political aspects. In their economic aspects they were seen as "agrarian empires" whose regimes acted as "revenue pumps," stifling any potential for cumulative economic and technological progress through the mechanism of rent-seeking. They were, moreover, seen like a raft on a largely unchanging, largely autarkic economy.

If that were so, the interweaving of state formation with the division of labor, urbanization, monetarization, and so on might be expected to be weaker and more narrowly confined. Does that mean that they were weaker in their cultural and psychological effects? Perhaps. The nearest European parallel to these regimes might be the estate system of the Middle Ages, when, as Elias suggested, modes of thought, feeling, and behavior remained more similar between members of the same estate across Europe than they were, for example, between warriors and townspeople who were geographical neighbors.

Opinion now is that even the Indian caste system allowed greater mobility, and greater diffusion and emulation of cultural traits, than was once thought. In any case, even if village India and China remained largely untouched by changes taking place in towns and courts, that does not make them so very different from rural Europe—Eugen Weber (1976) has, for instance, argued that many modern traits, even including the use of the fork at table, reached remoter parts of France only in the second half of the nineteenth century. And Eric Dunning and his collaborators (1988) have shown how even today lower-class groups in Britain vary in the degree of their exposure to civilizing pressures.

Be that as it may, the Song period in China and the Tokugawa period in Japan—both often described as "early modern"—exhibit many symptoms resembling those of the European civilizing process.

The Song era, as Eric Jones discussed in chapter 5 above, was one in which China achieved *intensive* economic growth—that is, self-sustained cumulative growth with rising per capita incomes. Jones points to the Song period as a theoretically highly significant counterbalance to traditional Industrial Revolution studies (and, broadly speaking, also the sociological tradition) which emphasize the "uniqueness of the West." In Song China, as in early modern Europe, especially France, courtiers and scholars regarded commerce as vulgar and demeaning, yet in rapidly growing metropolitan centers trade and industry prospered. Again as in Europe, it looks as though the "pressure from below" of an expanding and increasingly prosperous commercial middle class upon the aristocratic circles above them helped to generate a refined courtly culture of music, painting, poetry, and cuisine. It is also notable that pastimes related to the arts of war, such as horsemanship, hunting, and polo, declined in favor of intricate, restrained, and "gentle" games and hobbies (cf. Elias and Dunning 1986).

The intensive growth of the Song age was stopped in its tracks by the Mongol invasion, and although the Mongols quickly absorbed much of Chinese culture and although there was great institutional continuity, China lapsed back into extensive growth, interspersed with periods when centrifugal forces were dominant and central administration relatively ineffective. The post-Song age is, however, of considerable interest in relation to Elias's theory, because there does seem to be an implicit link between intensifying civilizing pressures and intensive economic growth—probably mediated through increased social mobility and the reconstruction of governing elites such as Elias points to as a key feature of the Renaissance period in Europe. I also think there are elements in Elias's arguments which may suggest that the intensity of civilizing pressures is related not (or *not only*) to the *extent* of webs of social interdependence, but to the *rate of change* and increase of social interdependencies. If that proves on further investigation to be the case, it raises the interesting possibility that a slowing of the rate of change (for example, a slowing of economic growth without an actual decline in per capita incomes) would be enough to precipitate a diminution of civilizing pressures or even the onset of decivilizing processes. But this is highly speculative.

Tokugawa Japan offers many parallels to Song China. In spite of the closure of Japan to the outside world, and the formal closure of Japanese social structure into four classes, in fact the period saw the rise of a vigorous merchant class, vibrant urban lifestyles, and more social mobility than was officially possible. Ikegami shows how changing power ratios between classes were expressed through fashions and sumptuary regulations, and how hierarchical norms and politeness spread through the transmission of samurai etiquette and manners to the merchant class. "Civilizing offensives" by upper-class groups toward the lower were much in evidence.[6] Ikegami produces clear evidence of the operation in Japan of the dialectical mechanism described by Elias as "colonization" and "repulsion," processes which produce something more complex than a simple "trickle-down" of cultural traits. An element of "trickle-up" is plainly evident in the much remarked success of the samurai class in taking to large-scale commerce after the Meiji Restoration.

But however difficult it may be to compare the diffusion of cultural traits up and down the social hierarchy and changes in outward ways of demanding and rendering respect between East and West, that task is a good deal easier than comparing the underlying psychogenetic changes, or changes in habitus, with which Elias was more fundamentally concerned. We cannot be surprised that nuances in the use of chopsticks in China serve some of the functions of table manners in Europe (Cooper 1986). Nor is it surprising that as early as the T'ang period there were books on verbal etiquette which remind one of Elias's discussion of "the modeling of speech at court" in France (Elias 1994, 88–93). But in the absence of long series and consecutive editions of manners books equivalent to those from which Elias felt able to draw strong conclusions about long-term changes in habitus, it is hard to make confident statements about equivalent processes in Asia. I am thinking of processes like the increasing social constraint toward self-constraint, the advance of thresholds of repugnance, shame, and embarrassment, pressures toward greater foresight, increasing rationalization, psychologization, and mutual identification.

Psychogenetic Changes, or Changes in Habitus

There are, however, many more isolated bits of evidence which are suggestive of counterparts to European civilizing processes. Sadler (1937, 389–90) quotes Tokugawa Ieyasu, the founder of the Tokugawa shogunate, as saying:

> The strong manly ones in life are those who understand the meaning of the word Patience. Patience means restraining one's inclinations. There are seven emotions: joy, anger, anxiety, love, grief, fear, and hate, and if a man does not give way to these he can be called patient. I am not as strong as I might be, but I have long known and practised patience. And if my descendants wish to be as I am . . . they must study patience.

Whether or not the samurai ethic, *Bushido,* can be shown to have a precisely similar range of connotations and social functions as the European notions of civility and civilization, it is probable that the development of any similar code involves increasing pressures toward self-constraint, at least among the class in which it develops. Probably it has wider impact. Ikegami concludes that contemporary Japanese culture is based on two complementary ingredients, "honorable competition" and "honorable collaboration," interacting to produce a dominant cultural trait of "honorific individualism." Viewed from afar, that seems to involve some interesting similarities to the emergence of the modern individualistic mode of self-experience in the West but, viewed more closely, marked differences are plainly evident. Thus, while on the one hand we have to look for similar underlying social processes and not be too carried away by old Western perceptions of the Orient, it is equally important to be alive to the emergence of different cultural flavors from similar ingredients.

Science and Knowledge

It would be overambitious here to do more than mention in passing the question of whether Elias's theory of knowledge and the sciences, and the connection he makes with civilizing processes (Elias 1987a), bears up well in an Asian context. But there are good signs that it does so. In particular, Elias's theory of time and timing (1992), to which again the idea of increasing social interdependencies exerting increased pressure toward self-constraints is central, is highly consonant with Joseph Needham's (1965) rebuttal of the myth of the "timeless Orient."

Some Conceptual Difficulties of Comparison

Several difficult conceptual and methodological problems arise at the outset in any attempt to use and test the theory of civilizing processes in a large-scale and long-term cross-cultural context. They include:

The Problem of Eurocentrism

It is—at least in the present context—a weakness of *The Civilizing Process* that it is based entirely on European evidence. But it is not so much that the book is Euro*centric* as that it is *about* Europe. Elias, in fact, began the book with a long section examining how the word "civilization"—derived in the late eighteenth century from the word *civilité* used by courtiers to describe the elaborate manners in which they took such pride as the means by which they were distinguished from the lower orders—came to acquire a whole penumbra of value connotations expressing (in the end) all the ways in which European society as a whole perceived itself as superior to other cultures.

> This concept expresses the self-consciousness of the West. . . . It sums up everything in which Western society of the last two or three centuries believes itself superior to earlier societies or "more primitive" con-

temporary ones. By this term Western society seeks to describe what constitutes its special character and what it is proud of: the level of *its* technology, the nature of *its* manners, the development of *its* scientific knowledge or view of the world, and much more. (1994, 3)

However, argues Elias, by the nineteenth century, the ways people in the West used the *word* civilization showed that they had already largely forgotten the *process* of civilization: it was for them completed and taken for granted. At this stage, confident of the superiority of their own now *apparently* inherent and eternal standards, they wished only to "civilize" the natives of lands they were now colonizing and, for a time, the lower classes of their own society (1994, 85). Far from being blindly naive about these things, Elias devoted the first forty-one pages of *The Civilizing Process* to showing how the very notion of civilization originated in a polemical context in Western European society, and how the concept had been used to legitimate the dominance first of certain groups in European states and then, increasingly, of European society as a whole vis-à-vis non-European and especially so-called primitive societies. Nevertheless, he said, with his eyes wide open to the ethnocentric use of the word by natives of Europe, "The value judgements contained in such statements are obvious; the facts to which they relate are less so" (1994, 182). If Elias's work can be criticized at all on this score, it is because, having identified the underlying long-term social process of which the value-loadings around the word "civilization" are but one minor manifestation, he does not signal clearly when he stops using the word in its popular, value-polluted, meaning and when he is using it in his own technical sense—without the quotation marks, so to speak. Yet the distinction is always clear in context. This opening section of Elias's book plainly gives the lie to the accusation that he was blissfully unaware of the functions of the concept of "civilization" for Europeans, or of the processes of the social construction of related concepts like "orientalism," which Edward Said (1978), among others, was to describe much later. For Elias, such concepts were a very typical facet of the relations between more powerful established groups and less powerful outsider groups; that such concepts came under challenge in the present century is also to be seen as a typical manifestation of relatively more equal power ratios between such groups. Certainly the overwhelming dominance of European-type societies in the world as a whole gave these concepts particular significance in a particular phase of history. But the excessive credence given to Said's polemic surely misses the point:[7] the great historical cultures of Asia, and the upper classes within them especially, have also developed concepts more or less corresponding to the European notion of "civilization" (in the nontechnical sense), expressing their own sense of superiority to their own lower orders and to foreign "barbarian" outsiders.

The Problem of Cultural Relativism

Radical relativists such as the anthropologist Hans-Peter Duerr (1988, 1990, 1993) have argued that there never was any such thing as a "civilizing process," in the factual sense of a social process, in Europe or anywhere else. Collating a rather random mass of evidence concerning attitudes to nakedness, sexuality, obscenity, and violence in many societies and periods, Duerr claims to show that there is simply no pattern through time or space to the development of feelings toward these matters. As against this, I have argued elsewhere (Mennell 1991) that what I call "the quantum theory of taboo" expressed by Duerr (and more generally by structuralist anthropologists) is impossible to refute. If it is inherently untestable, then a theory such as that of civilizing processes, based on actual evidence of changes in behavior, is preferable because it is in principle capable of being tested and extended through careful comparison of sequences of change over time in different cultures. Nevertheless, there are some serious problems of intercultural comparison, the most important of which I call the problem of measuring rods.

The Problem of Measuring Rods

In fact, the theory of civilizing processes requires at least *two* measuring rods, for (to oversimplify again) it specifies a relationship between two sequential orders, broadly the sociogenetic and the psychogenetic. One might picture these as two axes of a graph. One scale or axis would concern the structure of development of social interdependencies, including the division of social functions and state formation. The second scale or axis would relate to the civilizing of behavior and changes in personality structure, so conceived of as a sequential order, in which development takes place in a discernible *direction*.

One test of the theory may then be thought of as involving the plotting of changes of personality structure and changes in social structure against each other on the relevant scales. Each plot would be dated,[8] and the more closely a regression line could be fitted, and the more consistently were later dates more distant from the origin than earlier ones, the better would it be for Elias's hypothesis. A random scatter of date plots would negate the theory.

Some care is required, however, in using this heuristic image of a graph. What Elias does in *The Civilizing Process,* figuratively if not literally, is to draw a graph of development within a single cultural area. In this case, the imaginary graph represents the track of development over time in European society. (Several different tracks would really be needed to cope with differences between regions and between strata.) He is concerned with a *sequence of changes* within a given social unit.

Something very different would be involved if an attempt were made to plot all the *different* cultures known to social scientists—tribal societies, ancient civilizations, contemporary nation-states—on a single graph. Such an exercise is just about conceivable using the Human Relations Area Files. But each of the plots of personality structure against social structural complexity would then represent a single static snapshot at one point in time. Bearing in mind the precise initial conditions Elias specifies for the process and how many variations he sees within the overall trend in Europe alone, it would be a very remarkable result indeed if an imaginary regression line fitted the plots for so many varied cultures snatched out of context in time as closely as those for Europe *through* history. Some of the plots would come from societies the circumstances of whose original development was in most respects very different from that of Western Europe; some from societies changing slowly and therefore in a short-term perspective not discernibly undergoing an actual civilizing process as societies; and still others from societies changing rapidly but under the modern worldwide globalizing impact of European-type societies. If such a regression line did emerge, it would represent not the track which a particular society had followed over time, but unwonted evidence of a more generally valid and "unilinear" track of general social development. This is unlikely.

Even calibrating our two imaginary measuring rods is not very easy. The sociogenetic or "structural" axis is the easier, and sociologists could probably agree on the main criteria. Elias himself (1983, 221) suggests four such criteria, all in need—he says—of refinement and more accurate calibration to facilitate comparisons.

1. The number of routine contacts that people of different classes, ages, and sex have at one stage of social development compared with another.
2. The number, length, density, and strength of chains of interdependence which individual people form within a time-space continuum at one stage of development compared with another.
3. The central balance of tensions in society: the number of power centers increases with a growing differentiation of functions, and inequality in the distribution of power decreases (without disappearing)—but Elias specifically says this criterion needs to be refined.
4. The level of controls (a) over extrahuman nature, (b) of people over each other, and (c) of each individual over him or herself.

The fourth criterion takes us into the field of Elias's theory of the growth of knowledge and the sciences, and also—point 4(c)—into the realm of our other, "psychogenetic," axis. (It should, however, be noted that while Elias believed these kinds of controls also changed in a characteristic way from stage to stage of social development, this pattern of change was "certainly not by a simple increase or decrease.")

Calibrating the hypothetical "psychogenetic" axis is altogether more difficult and controversial. What is required in order for changes in social behavior and personality structure to be represented on an ordinal scale, as a sequential order, as "earlier" and "later" stages of development? The first essential is that one can point to "things once allowed" that "are now reproved." To a determined relativist, that proves nothing, but I propose to ignore the "quantum theory of taboo." Even so, there are serious conceptual problems here. Obviously, in comparing major cultures, there would be superficial differences in the direction of changes in manners and social behavior. Developments in table manners toward the use of chopsticks in China rather than knives, forks, and spoons, or the persistence of eating with the fingers in India do not in themselves undermine Elias's thesis. What is needed, however, is a common measuring rod for underlying social psychological changes. In attempting to test Elias's theory cross-culturally, the problem is to show whether or not the basic shift in the balance between external constraints and self-constraints in the social habitus of individuals is correlated with the social webs becoming more extensive and complex. In more detail, the theory predicts that the operation of self-constraints will become *more automatic, more even* (meaning that oscillations of mood become less extreme and controls over emotional expression become more reliable or calculable), and more *all-embracing.*[9] The latter means a decline in the differences between various spheres of life, such as contrasts between what is allowed in public and in private, between conduct in relation to one category of people as against another, or between "normal" behavior and that permissible on special occasions like carnival, which are seen as exceptions to the rules. These questions are sociologically researchable—indeed they are being researched in a Western context by historians and sociologists of the emotions (see, for example, Stearns and Stearns 1986 and Kemper 1990)—but they are not easy ones. Especially for the notion of controls becoming "more automatic," one might wish to work with a conception of the changing distance traversed between the emotional condition of young children and the standards of control expected of adults. In psychoanalytic terms, one might speak of the "level of development of the superego." But these conceptions are inherently difficult and controversial (see Mennell 1989a, 228 ff.), and cultural relativists will see them as the beginnings of scaling people of different cultures as more or less civilized not only in the technical sense but also in the more Eurocentric and unacceptable sense of the term.

The Problem of Decivilizing Processes

As I emphasized in chapter 6, Elias never regarded the European civilizing process as having followed a straight line (still less did he see it as "progress"). Civilizing processes are reversible, and there are many counterspurts within the process, so that the main trend is visible only in the long view. The period over which he studied European manners books, from the late Middle Ages to the mid-nineteenth century, was in the broad view one in which the division of labor, economic growth, and state formation followed an upward trajectory. Nevertheless, in the late Middle Ages, while part of the old warrior class in Western Europe was being tamed and transformed into courtiers, other elements of the same class who were not caught up in courts actually became *more* violent and aggressive in their lifestyle under the pressure of the erosion of their social base (Maso 1982; Mennell 1989a, 80). As Goudsblom observes, "It may not be a bad rule of thumb and not an unsound research strategy to assume that for any given trend a counter-trend may be found, operating in the opposite direction" (page 26 above). What Elias does assert is that, in the *very* long term, integration processes have predominated over disintegration processes. The "survival units" in which humans live—inside which levels of violence are relatively low compared with violence between survival units—have become larger. Taagepera (1978) has demonstrated quantitatively how, after the collapse of each of the great empires in the Old World, the next succeeding one managed to integrate a larger geographical area than its precursor. And for all their prejudices against "progress theories," few sociologists or anthropologists doubt that on the whole more complex societies have arisen out of less complex. Nevertheless, as we have seen, in Japan, China, and India, there were considerable fluctuations in the balance between centrifugal and centripetal forces, as well as economic setbacks. A comparative study of Europe with these Asian societies therefore necessitates an investigation not just of civilizing processes but of decivilizing processes too.

Conclusions

This discussion has been mainly exploratory, but I hope it has succeeded at least in showing the potential interest of attempting to extend the theory of civilizing processes by systematically comparing the European experience with that of the great historic Asian cultures, and thereby in some respects to provide a test of the original theory.

In conclusion, it is worth commenting on how this approach may relate to older established research traditions in comparative-historical sociology. The two principal ones stem from Marx and from Weber. Both, in their different ways, have tended to foster Eurocentrism, or at least an implicit acceptance of the uniqueness of the European (including North American) historical experience. Marx did so by sidelining the "Asiatic mode of production" as something outside the sequence of development through feudalism to capitalism, which he saw as the standard—i.e., European—model. Debates have raged about this ever since and interlinked with discussions of "Oriental despotism" from the early nineteenth century to Wittfogel. Weber reinforced the same tendency by seeking through his studies in the social psychology of the world religions (1951, 1958, 1978) to isolate the novel cultural ingredient which had made the difference in Western Europe. Much subsequent research has been dominated by the search for one or another "propellant" in the rise of capitalism.

Although, as Goudsblom (1977, 188–89) has argued, Weber's *The Protestant Ethic* (1930 [1904–5]) is "a masterpiece of well-documented interpretative understanding," it is also hopelessly inconclusive when it comes to the problem of explaining the actual part played by Calvinism in the sociogenesis of capitalism. In spite of that, the Weber thesis has shored up the tendency of sociologists to treat Europe as a unique case.[10] It has also led to the pleasant pastime of looking for analogies to the Protestant ethic in the religions of Asia to account for localized or more general burgeonings of capitalism—Bellah's *Tokugawa Religion* (1957) is an apposite example in view of Japan's recent rise to economic dominance. At its worst, the risk with this concern with cultural ingredients in development is that it leads to a preoccupation with static characterizations of "national character."[11]

Of course, "uniqueness" is not a property inherent in the object, but an artifact of the level of conceptual abstraction at which sociologists choose to work—rather like photographs are a result of the photographer's choice of lens. Elias was especially good at using variable-focus lenses in order to balance the particular and the general, to uncover general underlying processes while remaining alive to variations of outcome peculiar to nations or groups within them. Although he was frequently criticized for neglecting the role of religion in civilizing processes—he discussed the Church mainly as an element in the play of power in the Middle Ages, not as a source of ethical influence—he would, I think, be prepared to see in the religions of Asia a major source at least of differently flavored outcomes to any civilizing processes discovered there. The erotic theme which entered Hindu society with Tantrism could hardly offer a better contrast with Calvinist asceticism. But, if Elias is right about the underlying connection between the web of social interdependencies and the psychogenetic component of civilizing processes, religious elements unlike those of Europe should not be enough on their own to stop a civilizing process in its tracks.

For the driving force of such processes lies not in "material" or "cultural" or other "factors," but in the unplanned but cumulative outcome of people's practical activities in coping with the environmental and social niches in which they find themselves. Goudsblom's notion of the "reception effect" (page 53 above) serves to remind us that social processes are not to be explained statically as the product of such-and-such percentage of this or that "factor," but as the result of the interweaving of the practical activities of interdependent people, unequal in power, over time. That, we would contend, is true of all the long-term processes discussed in this book—the domestication of fire, the transition to agrarian societies, and extensive and intensive growth, as well civilizing and decivilizing processes.

Notes

1. Apart from Ikegami and Arnason, who are mentioned below, Elçin Kürsat-Ahlers has produced a remarkable study of state formation among the early Eurasian nomads (1994), which is expressly designed as a test and elaboration of Elias's theory. In a completely different cultural context, that of the Canadian Inuit, Wim Rasing (1994) also critically employs the theory of civilizing processes.

2. In view of the debates about whether "feudalism" as it is understood in European history existed in Asia (see, for example, Coulborn 1956; J.W. Hall 1968; Duus 1969; Critchley 1978; Mukhia 1981), it is perhaps a little hazardous to use the word "feudalization" here. However, I am using it in a limited sense to mean a process of the fragmentation of effective rule to smaller territories dominated by warriors.

3. Johann Arnason (1994) disagrees with my interpretation here, seeing Japan, rather like China, as having existed for more than two millennia as a single continuous "imagined community." The difference between us may be related to my own particular interest in the psychogenetic effects of rising levels of danger, insecurity, and uncertainty in everyday life.

4. Goudsblom (1992, 142) mentions an interesting footnote to the story: the use of firearms was gradually restricted to the samurai, who then ceased almost entirely to use them, preferring in their struggles with each other to revert to the older arts of swordsmanship—the case seems to be an anticipation of the mutually expected self-restraint which has (so far) prevented the use of nuclear weapons.

5. Apart from *The Civilizing Process* itself, and especially the remarks in the conclusion to the whole work (1994, 513–24), see Elias's comments on the emergence of the British party system out of the fairly evenly balanced outcome of a cycle of violence in the seventeenth century (in Elias and Dunning 1986, 26–40; cf. Mennell 1989a, 90–92), as well as *The Germans* (Elias, 1996).

6. The term "civilizing offensives" is associated especially with the work of Goudsblom's fellow members of the Amsterdam school, who have used it in the study of a wide range of middle-class campaigns directed at workers and peasants (see Mennell 1989a, 121–25).

7. Said's work has itself more recently come under critical scrutiny. See, for example, Richardson (1990).

8. Here I do not mean literally dates in the sense of years B.C. or A.D., but rather time-lapse plots from whenever the particular civilizing process was observed to be under way. The underlying process is the concern.

9. The published translations of Elias use the less self-explanatory expression "more all-round."

10. This is evident, for example, in the work of Michael Mann (1986, 1993) and his associates (Hall 1985; Baechler, Hall, and Mann 1988); Mann follows a chapter comprising "a comparative excursus into the world religions" with three on "the European dynamic."

11. The concept of "habitus" (see above, p. 101) is now being employed in a re-examination of issues once discussed under the rubric of "national character"—its advantage being that it specifically involves a denial of any suggestion that "national character" is in any sense innate in the people of a country. Elias's *The Germans* (1996) is a good example of this new trend, as is Ikegami's *The Taming of the Samurai* (1995). Ikegami is surprisingly sympathetic to a famous classic of the "national character" literature, Ruth Benedict's celebrated *The Chrysanthemum and the Sword* (1946). She shares a contemporary Japanese estimate that Benedict pointed to something extremely important in the Japanese "keen sensitivity to shame and a corresponding concern for good reputation and honour," which "are still important factors in the daily life of the Japanese people" (Ikegami 1995, 18, 375–76).

It should be noted that Elias, unlike those of the culture and personality school in anthropology, never works with a static polarity of "shame" versus "guilt." Even though his notion of a shifting balance between external constraints and self-restraints has an affinity with psychoanalytic theories of shame and guilt, he always thinks in terms of *both* being present in a culture, and of a *process* of development tilting the balance between the two. E.R. Dodd, in his classic *The Greeks and the Irrational* (1951), uses ideas derived from Benedict and her associates, not from Elias, but uses them in a processual way to understand *changes* in Greek character in the course of social development. In *The Germans,* Elias investigates with some subtlety the development of German habitus in the context of power struggles in the nineteenth and twentieth century. On recent usage of the notion of "national character," see also Wilterdink (1993).

Bibliography

Abrams, Philip. 1982. *Historical Sociology*. Shepton Mallet, UK: Open Books.

Adams, Robert McC. 1966. *The Evolution of Urban Society: Early Mesopotamia and Prehispanic Mexico*. Chicago: Aldine.

Albrow, Martin, and Elizabeth King, eds. 1990. *Globalization*. London: Sage.

Anderson, Benedict. 1983. *Imagined Communities: Reflections on the Origins and Spread of Nationalism*. London: Verso.

Anderson, J.L. 1981. "Climatic Change in European Economic History." *Research in Economic History* 6: 1–34.

———. 1991. *Explaining Long-Term Economic Change*. London: Macmillan.

Anderson, Perry. 1974a. *Passages from Antiquity to Feudalism*. London: New Left Books.

———. 1974b. *Lineages of the Absolutist State*. London: New Left Books.

Arnason, Johann. 1994. "Elias in Japan: State Formation and Civilising Process on the Far Eastern Fringe." Paper presented at XIII World Congress of Sociology, Bielefeld, Germany, 18–23 July, Ad Hoc Group 11, "Figurational Sociology," session 2.

Azu, Noa Akunor Aguae. 1929. *Adangbe (Adangme) History*. Accra: Government Printing Office.

Baechler, J.; J.A. Hall, and M. Mann, eds. 1988. *Europe and the Rise of Capitalism*. Oxford, UK: Basil Blackwell.

Basu, K.; E.L. Jones, and E. Schlicht. 1987. "The Growth and Decay of Custom: The Role of the New Institutional Economics in Economic History." *Explorations in Economic History* 24, no. 1: 1–21.

Bax, Mart. 1988. *Religieuze Regimes in Ontwikkeling: Verhulde Vormen van Macht en Afhankelijkheid*. Hilversum, Netherlands: Gooi en Sticht.

Beckerman, W. 1974. *In Defence of Economic Growth*. London: Jonathan Cape.

Bellah, Robert N. 1957. *Tokugawa Religion*. Glencoe, IL: Free Press.

Benedict, Ruth. 1946. *The Chrysanthemum and the Sword*. Boston: Houghton Mifflin.

van Benthem van den Bergh, Godfried. 1992. *The Nuclear Revolution and the End of the Cold War: Forced Restraint*. London: Macmillan.

Bentley, Jerry. 1993. *Old World Encounters*. New York: Oxford University Press.

Bickerman, E.J. 1980. *Chronology of the Ancient World*. 2d ed. London: Thames and Hudson.

Bloch, Marc. 1966. *Land and Work in Medieval Europe*. New York: Harper & Row.

Blumer, Herbert. 1969. *Symbolic Interactionism: Perspective and Method*. Englewood Cliffs, NJ: Prentice-Hall.

Boserup, Ester. 1965. *The Conditions of Agricultural Growth*. Chicago: Aldine.

———. 1981. *Population and Technology*. Oxford, UK: Basil Blackwell.

Burke, Peter. 1992. *History and Social Theory*. Ithaca: Cornell University Press.

Butterfield, Herbert. 1981. *The Origins of History*. London: Methuen.

Cairns, E., and R. Wilson. 1985. "Psychiatric Aspects of Violence in Northern Ireland." *Stress Medicine* 1: 193-201.

Cameron, Rondo. 1970. "Europe's Second Thoughts." *Comparative Studies in Society and History* 12: 452-62.

Chandler, T., and G. Fox. 1974. *3000 Years of Urban Growth*. New York: Academic Press.

Chartier, Roger. 1985. "Text, Symbols and Frenchness: Historical Uses of Symbolic Anthropology." *Journal of Modern History* 57, no. 4: 682-95.

Chirot, Daniel. 1994. *How Societies Change*. Thousand Oaks, CA: Pine Forge Press.

Churchill, Winston S. 1930. *My Early Life*. London: Thornton Butterworth.

Clark, J.D., and J.W.K. Harris. 1985. "Fire and Its Roles in Early Hominid Lifeways." *The African Archaeologist* 3: 3-27.

Clark, Stuart. 1985. "The *Annales* Historians." In *The Return of Grand Theory in the Human Sciences*, ed. Q. Skinner. Cambridge: Cambridge University Press, 177-98.

Clastres, Pierre. 1980. *Recherches d'Anthropologie politique*. Paris: Editions du Seuil.

Clough, S.B. 1961. *The Rise and Fall of Civilization*. New York: Columbia University Press.

Collins, Randall. 1986. *Weberian Sociological Theory*. Cambridge: Cambridge University Press.

Conrad, Geoffrey W., and Arthur A. Demarest. 1984. *Religion and Empire: The Dynamics of Aztec and Inca Expansionism*. Cambridge: Cambridge University Press.

Cooper, Eugene. 1986. "Chinese Table Manners: You Are How You Eat." *Human Organisation* 45, no. 2: 179-84.

Coulborn, Rushton, ed. 1956. *Feudalism in History*. Princeton, NJ: Princeton University Press.

Critchley J. 1978. *Feudalism*. London: Allen and Unwin.

Crosby, A.W. 1986. *Ecological Imperialism: The Biological Expansion of Europe, 900–1900*. Cambridge: Cambridge University Press.

Curtin, P.D. 1984. *Cross-Cultural Trade in World History*. Cambridge: Cambridge University Press.

Darnton, Robert. 1984. *The Great Cat Massacre and Other Essays*. New York: Basic Books.

Dening, G.M. 1980. *Islands and Beaches: Discourse on a Silent Land, Marquesas 1774-1880*. Melbourne, Australia: Melbourne University Press.

Dodds, E.R. 1951. *The Greeks and the Irrational*. Berkeley: University of California Press.

Dodgshon, R.A. 1987. *The European Past*. London: Macmillan Education.

Drucker, P. 1987. "Japan's Choices." *Foreign Affairs* 65: 923-41.

Dublin, L.I.; A.J. Lotka, and M. Spiegelman, 1936. *Length of Life—A Study of the Life Table*. New York: The Ronald Press.

Duby, Georges. 1980. *The Three Orders: Feudal Society Imagined*. Chicago: University of Chicago Press.

Duerr, Hans-Peter. 1988, 1990, 1993. *Der Mythos vom Zivilisationsprozeß.* Vol. 1, *Nacktheit und Scham,* vol. 2, *Intimität,* vol. 3, *Obszönität und Gewalt.* Frankfurt, Germany: Suhrkamp.

Dunning, Eric. 1977. "In Defence of Developmental Sociology: A Critique of Popper's *Poverty of Historicism* with Special Reference to the Theory of Auguste Comte." *Amsterdams Sociologisch Tijdschrift* 4, no. 3: 327-49.

Durand, J.D. 1977. "Historical Estimates of World Population: An Evaluation." *Population and Development Review* 3: 253-96.

Duus, Peter. 1969. *Feudalism in Japan.* New York: Alfred A. Knopf.

Elias, Norbert. 1977. "Zur Grundlegung einer Theorie sozialer Prozeße," *Zeitschrift für Soziologie* 6, no. 2: 127-49.

————. 1978. *What is Sociology?* New York: Columbia University Press.

————. 1983. *The Court Society.* Oxford, UK: Basil Blackwell.

————. 1985. *Humana Conditio.* Frankfurt, Germany: Suhrkamp.

————. 1987a. *Involvement and Detachment.* Oxford, UK: Blackwell.

————. 1987b. "The Retreat of Sociologists into the Present." *Theory, Culture and Society* 4, no. 2-3: 223-48.

————. 1991. *The Symbol Theory.* London: Sage.

————. 1992. *Time: An Essay.* Oxford, UK: Blackwell.

————. [1939] 1994. *The Civilising Process.* Oxford, UK: Blackwell.

————. 1996 *The Germans: Power Struggles and the Development of Habitus in the Nineteenth and Twentieth Centuries.* Trans. Eric Dunning and Stephen Mennell. Cambridge: Polity Press.

Elias, Norbert, and Eric Dunning. 1986. *Quest for Excitement.* Oxford, UK: Basil Blackwell.

Elvin, Mark. 1973. *The Pattern of the Chinese Past.* London: Eyre Methuen.

Finley, M.I. 1977. *The World of Odysseus.* 2d ed. London: Chatto & Windus.

Fletcher, Jonathan. 1995. "Towards a Theory of Decivilising Processes." *Amsterdams Sociologisch Tijdschrift,* 22, no. 2: 283-96.

Fukuyama, Francis. 1992. *The End of History and the Last Man.* London: Hamish Hamilton.

Galloway, P.R. 1986. "Long-Term Fluctuations in Climate and Population in the Preindustrial Era." *Population and Development Review* 12: 1-24.

Geertz, Clifford. 1973. *The Interpretation of Cultures.* New York: Basic Books.

Gellner, Ernest. 1988. *Plough, Sword and Book: The Structure of Human History.* London: Collins Harvill.

Glassman, Ronald. 1986. *Democracy and Despotism in Primitive Societies: A Neo-Weberian Approach.* 2 vols. Millwood, N.Y.: Associated Faculty Press.

Glick, T.F. 1979. *Islamic and Christian Spain in the Early Middle Ages.* Princeton, NJ: Princeton University Press.

Goldsmith, R. 1987. *Premodern Financial Systems: A Historical Comparative Study.* Cambridge: Cambridge University Press.

Goldthorpe, John H. 1991. "The Uses of History in Sociology: Reflections on Some Recent Tendencies." *British Journal of Sociology* 42, no. 2: 211-30.

Gottwald, Norman K. 1979. *The Tribes of Yahweh: A Sociology of Liberated Israel 1250-1050 B.C.E.* Maryknoll, N.Y.: Orbis Books.

Goudsblom, Johan. 1980. 1977. *Sociology in the Balance.* Oxford, UK: Basil Blackwell.

———. [1960] 1980. *Nihilism and Culture.* Oxford, UK: Basil Blackwell.

———. 1984. "Die Erforschung von Zivilisationsprozeßen." In *Macht und Zivilisation,* ed. P.R. Gleichmann; J. Goudsblom, and H. Korte. Frankfurt, Germany: Suhrkamp, 129-47.

———. 1986. "The Human Monopoly on the Use of Fire: Its Origins and Conditions." *Human Evolution* 1: 517–23.

———. 1987. "The Domestication of Fire as a Civilizing Process." *Theory, Culture and Society,* 4, no. 2–3: 457–76.

———. 1989. "Stijlen en Beschavingen." *De Gids* 152: 720–22.

———. 1990. "The Impact of the Domestication of Fire upon the Balance of Power Between Human Groups and Other Animals." *Focaal* 13: 55–65.

———. 1992a. "The Civilizing Process and the Domestication of Fire." *Journal of World History* 3: 1–12.

———. 1992b. *Fire and Civilization.* London: Allen Lane The Penguin Press.

———. 1994. "The Theory of the Civilising Process and Its Dicontents." Papers in progress, Amsterdam School for Social Science Research. Paper presented at the XIII World Congress of Sociology, Bielfeld, Germany, 18–23 August, Ad Hoc Group 11, session 1.

Goudsblom, Johan, and Stephen Mennell. Forthcoming 1996. "Civilizing Processes—Myth or Reality?" Contribution to review symposium on Hans-Peter Duerr, *Der Mythos vom Zivilisationsprozeße,* in *Comparative Studies in Society and History.*

Guha, A.S. 1981. *An Evolutionary View of Economic Growth.* Oxford, UK: Clarendon Press.

Halbwachs, Maurice. 1950. *La Mémoire collective.* Paris: Presses Universitaires de France.

Hall, John A. 1985. *Powers and Liberties: The Causes and Consequences of the Rise of the West.* Oxford, UK: Basil Blackwell.

Hall, John W. 1968. "Feudalism in Japan: A Reassessment." In *Studies in the Institutional History of Early Modern Japan,* ed. J.W. Hall and M.B. Jansen. Princeton, NJ: Princeton University Press.

Hallpike, C.R. 1986. *The Principles of Social Evolution.* New York: Oxford University Press.

Harris, Marvin. 1968. *The Rise of Anthropological Theory.* New York: Columbia University Press.

———. 1974. *Cows, Pigs, Wars, and Witches: The Riddle of Culture.* New York: Random House.

———. 1977. *Cannibals and Kings: The Origins of Cultures.* New York: Random House.

———. 1985. *Good to Eat: Riddles of Food and Culture.* New York: Simon & Schuster.

———. 1993. *Culture, People, Nature: An Introduction to General Anthropology.* 6th ed. New York: Harper & Row.

Harris, Marvin, and Eric B. Ross. 1987. *Death, Sex, and Fertility: Population Regulation in Preindustrial and Developing Societies.* New York: Columbia University Press.

Hirschman, A.O. 1985. *A Bias for Hope*. Boulder, CO., and London: Westview Encore.

Hopkins, Keith. 1978. *Conquerors and Slaves: Sociological Studies in Roman Society*. Vol. 1. Cambridge: Cambridge University Press.

Hosin, A.A. 1983. "The Impact of International Conflict on Children's and Adolescents' National Perceptions." Ph.D. diss., University of Ulster.

Huber, Hugo. 1963. *The Krobo: Traditional Social and Religious Life of a West African People*. St. Augustin nahe Bonn, Germany: Anthropos Institute.

Ikegami, Eiko. 1995. *The Taming of the Samurai: Honorific Individualism and the Making of Modern Japan*. Cambridge, MA: Harvard University Press.

Ingold, Tim. 1986. *Evolution and Social Life*. Cambridge: Cambridge University Press.

Isaac, Rhys. 1983. *The Transformation of Virginia 1740-1790*. Chapel Hill: University of North Carolina Press.

Jackson, R.H. 1987. "Quasi-States, Dual Regimes, and Neoclassical Theory: International Jurisprudence and the Third World." *International Organization* 41: 519–49.

Jacobsen, Thorkild. 1939. *The Sumerian King List*. Chicago: University of Chicago Press.

James, Steven R. 1989. "Hominid Use of Fire in the Lower and Middle Pleistocene." *Current Anthropology* 30: 1–26.

Johnson, Allen W., and Timothy Earle. 1987. *The Evolution of Human Societies: From Foraging Group to Agrarian State*. Stanford, CA: Stanford University Press.

Jones, E.L. 1982. "No Stationary State: The World Before Industrialisation." Workshop in Economic History, Department of Economics, University of Chicago, 8283–89.

———. 1985. *"Very* Long-Term Economic Development as the History Survey." Economics Discussion Papers, no. 2/85. Bundoora, Victoria, Australia: School of Economics, La Trobe University.

———. [1981] 1987. *The European Miracle: Environments, Economies, and Geopolitics in the History of Europe and Asia*. 2d ed. Cambridge: Cambridge University Press.

———. 1988. *Growth Recurring: Economic Growth in World History*. Oxford, UK: Clarendon Press.

———. 1989. Review of *The Collapse of Complex Societies*, by J.A. Tainter. *Economic History Review*, 2d ser., 42: 634.

———. 1990a. "A New Political History of Economic Growth." *Policy* 6, no. 1: 59–61.

———. 1990b. "The Real Question About China: Why Was the Song Economic Experiment Not Repeated?," *Australian Economic History Review* 30: 5–22.

Jones, E.L.; L.E. Frost, and C.M. White. 1993. *Coming Full Circle: An Economic History of the Pacific Rim*. Boulder, CO: Westview Press.

Jones, S.R.H. 1988. "Economic Growth and the Spread of the Market Principle in Later Anglo-Saxon England." University of Auckland Working Papers in Economics, no. 48.

Kaufmann, Walter, ed. 1968. *Basic Writings of Nietzsche*. New York: Random House.

Keene, D. 1969. *The Japanese Discovery of Europe: Honda Toshiaki and Other Discoveries 1720–1798*. Stanford, CA: Stanford University Press.

Keynes, John Maynard. 1951. *Essays in Persuasion.* London: Rupert Hart-Davis.

Kilminster, Richard. Forthcoming 1996. "Globalization as an Emergent Concept." In *The Limits of Globalization,* ed. Alan Scott. London: Routledge.

Konvitz, Josef W., ed. 1985. *What Americans Should Know: Western Civilisation or World History?* Lansing: Michigan State University Press.

Kuhn, Thomas S. 1970. *The Structure of Scientific Revolutions.* 2d ed. Chicago: University of Chicago Press.

Kuran, T. 1988. "The Tenacious Past: Theories of Personal and Collective Conservatism." *Journal of Economic Behavior and Organization* 10: 143–71.

Kürsat-Ahlers, Elçin. 1994. *Zur frühen Staatenbildung von Steppenvölkern: Über die Sozio- und Psychogenese der eurasischen Nomadenreiche am Beispiel der Hsiung-Nu und Göktürken mit einem Exkurs über die Skythen* (Early state formation among the peoples of the Steppes: On the sociogenesis and psychogenesis of the Eurasian Nomadic Empires, with reference to the Hsiung-Nu and with a digression on the Scythians). Berlin: Duncker & Humblot.

Ladurie, E. Le Roy. 1973. "Un Concept: l'unification microbienne du monde (XIV–XVII siecles)." *Revue Suisse d'Histoire* 23: 673–92.

Lenski, Gerhard. 1966. *Power and Privilege: A Theory of Social Stratification.* New York: McGraw-Hill.

Lewis, W. Arthur. 1955. *The Theory of Economic Growth.* London: George Allen and Unwin.

Lincoln, Bruce. 1981. *Priests, Warriors and Cattle: A Study in the Ecology of Religions.* Berkeley: University of California Press.

Lloyd, Seton. 1984. *The Archaeology of Mesopotamia.* 2d ed. London: Thames and Hudson.

McCormack, G. 1988. "Japan's Superpower Dilemmas." *Understanding Japan.* University of Adelaide Centre for Asian Studies Public Lecture Series: 3–13.

MacDonald, Michael D. 1983. *Children of Wrath: Political Violence in Northern Ireland.* Ph.D. diss., University of California, Berkeley.

McEvedy, C., and R. Jones. 1978. *Atlas of World Population History.* Harmondsworth, Middlesex, UK: Penguin Books.

Mackenzie, W.J.M. 1978. *Biological Ideas in Politics.* Harmondsworth, Middlesex, UK: Penguin Books.

MacMullen, Ramsay. 1974. *Roman Social Relations, 50 B.C. to A.D. 284.* New Haven, CT: Yale University Press.

McNeill, William H. 1963. *The Rise of the West: A History of the Human Community.* Chicago: University of Chicago Press.

———. [1976] 1979. *Plagues and Peoples.* Harmondsworth, Middlesex, UK: Penguin Books.

———. 1982. *The Pursuit of Power.* Chicago: University of Chicago Press.

———. 1984. "Human Migration in Historical Perspective." *Population and Development Review* 10: 1–18.

———. 1986. *Mythistory and Other Essays.* Chicago: University of Chicago Press.

Maddison, A. 1982. *Phases of Capitalist Development.* Oxford, UK: Oxford University Press.

Maine, Sir Henry. 1883. *Dissertations on Early Law and Custom.* London: John Murray.

Mann, Michael. 1986, 1993. *The Sources of Social Power.* Vol. 1, *A History of Power from the Beginning to A.D. 1760.* Vol. II, *The Rise of Classes and Nation-States, 1760–1914.* Cambridge: Cambridge University Press.

Maso, Benjo. 1982. "Riddereer en riddermoed—ontwikkelingen van de aanvalslust in de late middeleeuwen" (Knightly honor and knightly courage: Changes in fighting spirit in the late Middle Ages). *Sociologische Gids* 29, no. 3–4: 296–325.

Mayhew, Anne. 1987. "Culture: Core Concept Under Attack." *Journal of Economic Issues* 21: 587–603.

Menken, J., and S.C. Watkins. 1985. "Famines in Historical Perspective." *Population and Development Review* 11: 647–75.

Mennell, Stephen. 1974. *Sociological Theory: Uses and Unities.* London: Thomas Nelson.

———. 1989a. *Norbert Elias: Civilisation and the Human Self-Image.* Oxford, UK: Basil Blackwell. Rev. ed. published 1992, under title *Norbert Elias: An Introduction.*

———. 1989b. "The Sociological Study of History: Institutions and Social Development." In *What Has Sociology Achieved?* ed. C.G.A. Bryant and H. Becker London: Macmillan.

———. 1990a. "Decivilising Processes: Theoretical Significance and Some Lines of Research." *International Sociology* 5, no. 2: 205–23.

———. 1990b. "The Globalization of Human Society as a Very Long-Term Social Process." *Theory, Culture and Society* 7, no. 2–3: 359–71.

———. 1991. "Food and the Quantum Theory of Taboo." *Etnofoor* 4, no. 1: 63–77.

———. 1992. "Momentum and History." In *Culture and History,* ed. J.L. Melling and J. Barry. Exeter, UK: University of Exeter Press, 28–46.

Moore, Barrington, Jr. 1966. *Social Origins of Dictatorship and Democracy.* Boston: Beacon Press.

Mukhia, H. 1981. "Was There Feudalism in Indian History?" *Journal of Peasant Studies* 18, no. 3: 273–310.

Müller-Lyer, F. 1915. *Phasen der Kultur unde Richtungslinien des Fortschritts: Sociologische Überblicke.* München, Germany: Albert Langen.

Needham, Joseph. 1965. *Time and Eastern Man.* London: Royal Anthropological Occasional Paper no. 21.

Nisbet, Robert A. 1969. *Social Change and History.* New York: Oxford University Press.

Noakes, J., and G. Pridham, eds. *Nazism 1919–1945.* Vol. 3, *Foreign Policy, War and Racial Extermination.* Exeter, UK: University of Exeter Press.

Patel, S.J. 1964. "The Economic Distance between Nations: Its Origin, Measurement and Outlook." *Economic Journal* 74: 119–31.

Patnaik, Naveen. 1985. *A Second Paradise: Indian Courtly Life, 1590–1947.* Garden City, NY: Doubleday.

Perlès, Catherine. 1987. "La naissance du feu." *L'Histoire* 105 (December): 28–33.

Persson, K.G. 1988. *Pre-industrial Economic Growth.* Oxford, UK: Basil Blackwell.

Popper, Karl R. 1945. *The Open Society and its Enemies.* 2 vols. London: Routledge and Kegan Paul.

———. 1957. *The Poverty of Historicism.* London: Routledge and Kegan Paul.

Rasing, Wim. 1994. *"Too Many People": Order and Nonconformity in Igluling-miut Social Process.* Nijmegen: Catholic University of Nijmegen.

Reid, A. 1988. *Southeast Asia in the Age of Commerce 1450–1680.* Vol. 1, *The Lands Below the Winds.* New Haven, CT: Yale University Press.

Richardson, Michael. 1990. "Enough Said: Reflections on Orientalism." *Anthropology Today* 6, no. 4: 16-19.

Rozman, G. 1973. *Urban Networks in Ch'ing China and Tokugawa Japan.* Princeton, NJ: Princeton University Press.

Rüstow, Alexander. 1950. *Ortsbestimmung der Gegenwart. Eine universalgeschichtliche Kulturkritik.* Vol. 1, *Ursprung der Herrschaft.* Zürich: Eugen Rentsch.

Sadler, A.L. 1937. *The Making of Modern Japan.* London: Allen and Unwin.

Sagarra, Eda. 1977. *A Social History of Germany, 1648-1914.* London: Methuen.

Sahlins, Marshall. 1972. *Stone Age Economics.* Chicago: Aldine.

Said, Edward. 1978. *Orientalism.* New York: Pantheon.

Sanderson, Stephen K. 1990. *Social Evolutionism: A Critical History.* Oxford, UK: Blackwell.

Scarre, Chris, ed. 1988. *Past Worlds: The Times Atlas of Archaeology.* London: Times Books.

Singh, R.C.P. 1968. *Kingship in Northern India (ca. 600 A.D.–1200 A.D.).* Delhi: Motilal Banarsidass.

Sitwell, N.H.H. 1986. *Outside the Empire: The World the Romans Knew.* London: Paladin.

Smith, C.S. 1981. *A Search for Structure.* Cambridge, MA: MIT Press.

Spencer, Herbert. 1862. *First Principles.* New York: Appleton.

Spier, Fred. 1995. "Regimes as Structuring Principles for Big History." Paper presented at the Annual Conference of the World History Association, Florence, 22–25 June.

Stone, J., and S.J. Mennell, eds. 1980. *Alexis de Tocqueville on Democracy, Revolution and Society.* Chicago: University of Chicago Press.

Stover, Leon E., and Takeko Kawai Stover. 1976. *China: An Anthropological Perspective.* Pacific Palisades, CA: Goodyear.

de Swaan, Abram. 1988. *In Care of the State: Health Care, Education and Welfare in Europe and the USA in the Modern Era.* Cambridge: Polity Press.

Taagepera, Rein. 1978. "Size and Duration of Empires: Systematics of Size." *Social Science Research* 7: 108–27.

Taagepera, Rein, and B.N. Colby. 1979. "Growth of Western Civilization: Epicyclical or Exponential?" *American Anthropologist* 81: 907–12.

Tainter, Joseph A. 1988. *The Collapse of Complex Societies.* Cambridge: Cambridge University Press.

Tylecote, R.F. 1987. *The Early History of Metallurgy in Europe.* London: Longman.

Tylor, Edward B. 1871. *Primitive Culture.* Vol. 1, *The Origins of Culture.* Gloucester, MA: Smith.

Usher, D. 1973. "An Imputation to the Measure of Economic Growth for Changes in Life Expectancy." In *The Measurement of Economic and Social Performance,* ed. M. Moss. Conference in Income and Wealth, vol. 38. New York: National Bureau of Economic Research.

de Vries, J. 1984. *European Urbanization 1500–1800.* Cambridge, MA: Harvard University Press.

Wacquant, Loïc. 1992. "Décivilisation et diabolisation: la mutation du ghetto noir américain." In *L'Amérique des français,* ed. T. Bishop and Christiane Faure. Paris: Editions François Bourin.

Wallace, A.R. 1962. *The Malay Archipelago.* New York: Dover.

Wallerstein, Immanuel. 1974, 1980, 1989. *The Modern World-System,* Vols. 1, 2, 3. New York: Academic Press.

Weber, Alfred. 1935. *Kulturgeschichte als Kultursoziologie.* Leiden: Sijthoff.

Weber, Eugen. 1976. *Peasants into Frenchmen: The Modernization of Rural France, 1870–1914.* Stanford, CA: Stanford University Press.

Weber, Max. [1904–5] 1930. *The Protestant Ethic and the Spirit of Capitalism.* London: Allen and Unwin.

———. 1951. *The Religion of China.* Glencoe, IL: Free Press.

———. 1958. *The Religion of India.* Glencoe, IL: Free Press.

———. [1896] 1976. "The Social Causes of the Decline of Ancient Civilisation." In *The Agrarian Sociology of Ancient Civilisations.* London: New Left Books, 389-411.

———. [1922] 1978. *Economy and Society.* 2 vols. Berkeley: University of California Press.

Wenke, Robert J. 1984. *Past Worlds: Humankind's First Three Million Years.* 2d ed. New York: Oxford University Press.

West, M.L. 1978. *Hesiod: Works and Days.* Oxford, UK: Clarendon Press.

Wichers, A.J. 1965. *De Oude Plattelandsbeschaving: Een Sociologische Bewustwording van de Overherigheid.* Assen, Netherlands: Van Gorcum.

Wilson, Bryan. 1975. *The Noble Savages: The Primitive Origins of Charisma and Its Contemporary Survival.* Berkeley: University of California Press.

Wilterdink, Nico. 1993. "An Examination of European and National Identity." *Archives européennes de sociologie* 34, no. 1: 119–36.

Wittfogel, Karl A. [1957] *Oriental Despotism: A Comparative Study of Total Power.* 2d ed. New York: Random House.

Wolf, Eric R. 1959. *Sons of the Shaking Earth: The People of Mexico and Guatemala.* Chicago: University of Chicago Press.

———. 1982. *Europe and the People Without History.* Berkeley: University of California Press.

Yoshihara, Kunio. 1986. *Japanese Economic Development.* Tokyo: Oxford University Press.

Zhou Linong. 1990. State Relief and Population Growth in Late Imperial China. Ph.D. diss., La Trobe University, Bundoora, Victoria, Australia.

———. 1993. "Effects of Government Intervention on Population Growth in Imperial China." *Journal of Family History* 18: 213–30.

Index

T

Taagepera, Rein, 28, 65, 72, 75–76, 131

Taboos, 45, 54

Tainter, Joseph A., 73, 113–14

Taming of the Samurai, The (Ikegami), 120, 134n.11

T'ang period, 118, 124

Third Estate, 55

Thucydides, 17, 19

Time: An Essay (Elias), 40–41

Time grid, objective, 18

Tokugawa, Ieyasu, 124

Tokugawa period, 85, 87, 88, 97–99, 119–20, 122, 123

Tokugawa Religion (Bellah), 132

Toqueville, Alexis de, 107

Toshiaki, Honda, 97

Trends, 27–28, 32–33
  countervailing, 54
  universal, 26

Triad of basic controls (Elias concept), 39

Turning point, 22, 23

Tylor, Edward, vii, 19, 21
  theory of stages, 31

U

Überlagerung process, 57

Urbanization, 71–72

W

Van Benthem van den Bergh, Godfried, 110

Vietnam War, 9–10

Vijayanga empire, 118

Violence, stages in monopolization of, 54–60, 61–62n.4
  forging of metals and, 56
  professional warrior class, 55–61
  restrictions on women, 54
  see also War; Warriors

Wacquant, Loïc, 113

Wallace, Alfred Russel, 96

Wallerstein, Immanuel, 9

War
  countermovements of, 32
  increasing scale of, 109
  as inherent tendency, 32
  see also Violence, stages in monopolization of; Warriors

Warring States period, 119

Warriors
  Angriffslust in, 109
  coalition between priests and, 59–60
  courtization of, 119–21
  peasants and, 57, 62n.8
  priesthood and, 59–60
  rise of, 33
  as Second Estate, 55
  sociogenesis of, 5, 33, 39, 50
  taming of, 119–21
  see also Military-agrarian regimes

About the Authors

Johan Goudsblom is Professor of Sociology at the University of Amsterdam. He studied at Wesleyan University, Middletown, Conn., and the University of Amsterdam, Netherlands. He has been a Visiting Fellow at Princeton, Berkeley, and All Souls College, Oxford, and a Visiting Professor at Konstanz and Exeter. His publications in English include *Dutch Society* (Random House, 1967), *Sociology in the Balance* (Blackwell, 1977), *Nihilism and Culture* (Blackwell, 1980), and *Fire and Civilization* (Penguin, 1992). His two most recent books in Dutch are collections of essays on the sociology of Norbert Elias (1987) and on language and social reality (1988).

Eric Jones is Professor Emeritus at La Trobe University and Professorial Associate of the Graduate School of Management, University of Melbourne, Australia. He is a Fellow of the Academy of the Social Sciences in Australia. He has been Visiting Professor of Economic History at the University of Exeter and the University of California, Davis. He has also taught at Oxford, Reading, Northwestern, Purdue, and Yale, and been a member of the Institute for Advanced Study at Princeton. He has published two books on very long-term change in large systems, *The European Miracle* (Cambridge University Press, 1981, 2d ed. 1987) and *Growth Recurring* (Oxford University Press, 1988), and is joint author of *Coming Full Circle* (Westview Press, 1993).

Stephen Mennell is Professor of Sociology in the National University of Ireland, and Head of the Department of Sociology at University College Dublin. From 1990 to 1993 he was Professor of Sociology at Monash University, Melbourne, Australia, and before that Reader in Sociology and Comparative European Studies at the University of Exeter, England. He read economics at Cambridge and has been Frank

Knox Fellow in the Department of Social Relations at Harvard and a Fellow of the Netherlands Institute for Advanced Study, Wassenaar. He is a Fellow of the Royal Historical Society. His three most recent books are *All Manners of Food* (Blackwell, 1985), *Norbert Elias: Civilisation and the Human Self-Image* (Blackwell, 1989), and *The Sociology of Food: Eating, Diet and Culture* (Sage, 1992).